ROTTWEILER

SMART OWNER'S GUIDE®

By Elaine Waldorf Gewirtz

FROM THE EDITORS OF
DOGFANCY® MAGAZINE

CONTENTS

Rottweiler, a Smart Owner's Guide®

ISBN: 978-1-593787-81-3 (Hardcover) ©2012

ISBN: 978-1-593787-93-6 (Softcover) ©2012

All rights reserved. No part of this book may be reproduced in any form, by Photostat, scanner, microfilm, xerography, or any other means, or incorporated into any information retrieval system, electronic or mechanical, without the written permission of the copyright owner.

photographers include Isabelle Francais/I-5 Publishing; Tara Darling/I-5 Publishing; Gina Cioli/I-5 Studio; Shutterstock.com

For CIP information, see page 176.
Printed in China.

If you are bringing a Rottweiler into your home from a responsible breeder or a rescue group, congratulations! You have chosen a strong, loyal, discerning breed that is loved and admired throughout the world. Ironically, the Rottweiler is also one of the most misunderstood and maligned breeds. Rottweilers serve as a perfect example of the damage that can be done to a fine breed's reputation when inappropriate owners are drawn to the wrong dog, neglect his socialization and training, then dispose of the dog when he becomes a burden. Confident, well-behaved Rottweilers in the company of their proud, responsible owners demonstrate to the world what a great breed this can be in the right hands.

It is believed that the Rottweiler descends from the drover dogs of ancient Rome. The dogs traveled with the armies, keeping the herds of cattle intact to feed the troops during their long marches. At night, the dogs guarded the supplies. By the middle of the twelfth century, increased commerce in cattle meant that butchers required dogs to drive the herds to and from market. Rottweilers performed this role admirably until the middle of the nineteenth century, at which time cattle driving was outlawed. This had a profound effect on the breed, and the number of Rottweilers diminished significantly. By 1901, the Rottie had found a new calling as a police dog in Germany.

The same versatility that the breed demonstrated then impresses us today. Rottweilers are at home in both country and city settings, protecting children, pulling carts, herding stock for farmers, and assisting police. To do this, however, the Rottweiler must be calm, brave, and confident without being unnecessarily aggressive. The American Kennel Club breed

The Rottweiler has plenty of herding instinct and ability for working with livestock.

standard states that the Rottweiler should respond "quietly and with a wait-and-see attitude to influences in his environment." Adaptability is important in the breed.

Unlike glamorous breeds with abundant coats to groom and style, the Rottweiler has a classic look. The breed is medium-large in size, robust, and powerful. The Rottie's coat is straight, coarse, dense, and always black in color, with markings in rust to mahogany. The head is broad; the expression is "noble, alert, and self-assured." The neck is moderately long and well muscled; the chest is broad and deep. The Rottweiler trots with strong reach in front and powerful drive in the rear.

The Rottweiler standard does not penalize an aloof or reserved dog, as this reflects the character of the breed, nor does the standard fault an aggressive or belligerent attitude toward other dogs, something of which pet owners need to be aware. This is not a breed that lends itself to immediate friendships; however, a shy Rottweiler or one who appears unwilling to be approached must be excused from the show ring. The standard illustrates the ideal temperament of the breed. The Rottweiler is a hard, dominant dog, but he must be calm and dependable. Edginess and fearfulness are not appropriate traits for the breed.

Conscientious breeders socialize their Rottweilers from puppyhood on to be stable companions. Breed rescue groups must monitor the Rotties in their care, particularly the adult dogs, to ensure that they can cope with the rigors of life in active new households. The rescue group

JOIN OUR ONLINE Club Rottie™

With this Smart Owner's Guide®, you are well on your way to earning your Rottweiler diploma. But your Rottie education doesn't end here. You are invited to join **Club Rottie™ (DogChannel.com/Club-Rottie)**, a FREE online site with lots of fun and instructive features, such as:

◆ **forums, blogs,** and **profiles** where you can connect with other Rottweiler owners

◆ **downloadable charts** and **checklists** to help you be a smart and loving dog owner

◆ access to Rottweiler **e-cards** and **wallpapers**

◆ interactive **games**

◆ canine **quizzes**

The **Smart Owner's Guide** series and **Club Rottie** are backed by the experts at DOG FANCY® magazine and DogChannel.com—who have been providing trusted and up-to-date information about dogs and dog people for more than forty years. Log on and join the club today!

from whom you adopt your Rottie should be able to tell you if a particular dog is trustworthy around children, men, women, and other pets.

Allan Reznik
Editor-at-Large, DOG FANCY

PROTECTOR

AND PAL

When a robust black dog appears on the scene, people take notice. Majestic, strong, and medium-large in size, the Rottweiler cuts an impressive figure. The courageous nature of a Rottweiler implies unquestionable protection. From the breed's roots as a noble guardian with a sweet temperament to its status as one of the most popular breeds in America, it's no surprise that you are interested in adding this black-and-rust beauty to your life.

Eager to protect those he loves, the Rottweiler has a solid-gold heart and a calm confidence. Add to that his dark brown eyes and self-assured gaze that stares into your soul, and it's no wonder that admirers fall fast for him. Underneath the breed's handsome good looks lies a loyal dog who can both act the clown and stand by his family without batting an almond-shaped eye.

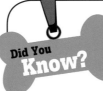

Did You Know?

A Rottweiler with good hips can easily leap over a 6-foot fence, but he won't make the leap without having a good reason. Boredom and something enticing on the other side are the usual motivators. Reputable Rottweiler breeders and rescue groups will not place a dog in a household that does not have a secure yard enclosure of at least 6 feet in height.

This versatile working breed is highly intelligent, strong-willed, and noble. He serves society in a variety of roles by assisting in search and rescue operations, working alongside patrol and drug-detection officials, and providing comfort as a therapy and assistance dog. When ethical breeders value good health, temperament, working ability, and conformation above all else, this trustworthy companion is one of dogdom's best-kept secrets.

Well-bred Rotties are not nervous or hyper. They are powerful dogs meant for endurance; thus they need a job to do and rules to follow. When they're not given basic training or occupied with activities, such as competitive sports, herding, or therapy work, Rottweilers can become big bullies rather than the guardians they were bred to be. Think of a two-year-old whose parents allow him to run amok with no discipline and without teaching him how to behave politely. Dogs who have not received proper training from their owners are probably the reason behind the breed's bad-boy reputation. While every dog needs training and a responsible owner, this is especially critical for Rottweilers, because the breed is often the target of breed-specific legislation.

With this in mind, Rotties may not be the best choice for first-time dog owners. They deserve to live in homes with people who understand the challenges of the breed and will commit to training and socializing their dogs the right way.

At the end of the day, a Rottweiler is all about companionship. From couch potato to athlete to protector, this breed is ready, willing, and able to be your best friend.

WHO SHOULD OWN A ROTTWEILER?
The right owners for a Rottie are those who will give their dog the opportunity to fulfill his impressive heritage. Consider the following types of Rottie owners to help you find out if you and the breed are a good match.

Up-for-a-challenge trainers: Rottweilers are brainiacs. There is little they can't learn, so their minds must be stimulated. When it comes to sizing up a situation or understanding what their owners are saying, Rotties stand at the top of the canine intelligence chart. Capable of recognizing hundreds of words and following dozens of commands, a Rottweiler thrives when he has a chance to use his noodle.

Can you stand to live with a dog who may outsmart you from time to time? A Rottweiler requires an owner who values his dog's sharp mind and enjoys the challenges of training.

Let's say that your dog becomes obsessed with a toy, and you decide to take it away and put it on top of a counter. Leave it to a Rottie to jump up and retrieve it or figure out how to climb onto a nearby chair for a boost. Not everyone appreciates a problem-solving dog, so give this some thought before acquiring a Rottie. Living with a Rottweiler may be challenging at times, but it will always be interesting.

Good disciplinarians: All dogs need rules and someone to take charge. This is especially true for Rottweilers, who can grow to weigh around 100 pounds and who may try to bully their owners if not taught right from wrong. The breed requires consistent day-to-day discipline. It's vital to obedience-train and socialize your Rottie at a young age and to learn how to handle his behavior while he is still small and you can remain in physical control.

Providing authoritative training doesn't mean exerting extreme or forceful behavior; rather, it means giving your dog fair

Many Rottweiler owners go beyond basic training and participate with their dogs in organized sports, such as competitve obedience.

and firm discipline and establishing steady leadership with patience and positive reinforcement. Once your dog accepts your position as the pack leader, he will respect you and your surroundings and will come to your aid when you need it. If you are fearful or timid around dogs, then owning this breed is not for you.

Active accomplices: On the day you bring your Rottie home, prepare to lace up your athletic shoes and burn some calories. Puppies and older dogs alike will need multiple short walks each day, but adult Rotties also require regular daily outings to get some real exercise. Swimming, walking, hiking, and jogging help keep your dog mentally and physically fit. If you prefer organized canine sports, such as agility, obedience, herding, tracking, or carting, your dog will benefit from the training and activity involved.

A tired Rottweiler is a well-behaved Rottweiler. If your dog expends some energy with you when you're home, he'll gladly sleep the time away when you're gone. Include your dog in your life as much as you can to stave off boredom and keep him from turning to unacceptable activities such as digging, barking, and chewing.

Don't let bad weather throw off your exercise routine. This is a double-coated breed—the Rottweiler has a soft undercoat and a coarse top coat. From his ancestral days spent living outdoors guarding cattle, the Rottweiler developed a protective outer coat to help insulate him in rain and snow. The coat dries quickly when wet, which is good because the typical Rottie likes water and thinks that getting wet is a lot of fun.

The Rottweiler isn't a breed that you can let loose while on a walk or at a dog beach or dog park. In these situations, the Rottie's protective nature and high prey instinct kicks into overdrive, and the dog can become possessive of the territory around him. Rotties are not afraid of cars or traffic either, and will think nothing of running into the street or going to explore a few blocks away.

Calm, cool companions: Although the Rottweiler requires exercise and activities, he also needs quiet time with his owner. While you must keep your Rottie active, don't think that wrestling, playing tug-of-war, or encouraging your dog to chase you is a good idea. These rambunctious play activities will only incite your Rottie to use his strength to overpower you and possibly even play-bite.

Well-bred Rotties are stable and mellow. Reputable breeders have dedicated their efforts to producing even-tempered dogs, and your interactions with your Rottweiler should match his energy level.

Don't expect a watchdog, either, even though the breed's size alone will discourage intruders. Rotties are noisy only when they need to be. They are generally quiet if someone comes to the door or shows up on your property, yet they're intelligent enough to sense if someone shouldn't be there—that's when their natural guarding

Did You Know?

During their first year, Rottweiler puppies are happy-go-lucky and eager to please their new owners. From around fourteen to eighteen months to two years of age, they become more active and may assert some independence and develop same-sex aggression.

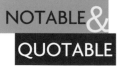

NOTABLE & QUOTABLE

Stable. That's the one word that best describes the Rottweiler's temperament. The dog isn't overtly friendly or overtly aggressive with strangers. He should have an even-keel, stable temperament and, when bred correctly, is definitely not an aggressive dog. He's loyal to his family and so versatile. A Rottweiler can learn whatever his owners want to teach him.

— Jeff Shaver, president of the American Rottweiler Club, from Magnolia, Texas

instinct to protect those they feel a bond with will prompt them to sound an alarm and make a fuss.

Bump-proof adults: Rottweiler owners should feel sturdy on their feet. A legacy from their cattle-herding days, Rottweilers have a natural tendency to herd those they love, which could result in someone accidentally being knocked over; children and frail adults are especially at risk.

So-so housekeepers: It's a fact. The Rottweiler, like many breeds, sheds his straight, medium-length coat twice a year. The rest of the time, it's not unusual to find straggler hairs scattered around the house. If black hairs collecting at the baseboards of your floors, showing up on your light-colored clothing, and floating onto your bedspreads and couch pillows don't annoy you, consider a Rottweiler.

Shedding or not, you will need to maintain your Rottie's overall condition with regular grooming. Brush your Rottie once a week—more often during times of shedding. Regularly brushing out the dead hair minimizes shedding by keeping the hair from falling out on its own inside the house. To keep his coat in good condition and free of odor, bathe your dog once a month.

Your Rottie's teeth should be brushed once a day to prevent dental disease. Nails grow quickly and should be trimmed weekly. Develop the habit of looking in your dog's ears every few days to make sure that they are clean and odor-free.

Establishing these spruce-up tasks as part of your routine gives you a good chance to bond with your dog. While you're at it, check him over for any scratches or lumps that may need medical attention.

BREED ATTITUDES

Like people, Rottweilers can have a range of temperaments, but conscientious breeders who care about the dogs that they produce always aim for calm, gentle, and stable Rottie puppies. A Rottweiler with the correct temperament is a confident and courageous dog. He tends to remain aloof with people he doesn't know, but aloof does not mean fearful. A Rottie with the correct temperament is reserved, proud, and independent but will accept what his owner wants, whether or not he enjoys it.

The Rottie's reserved nature doesn't translate to forming an immediate friendship with someone he meets for the first time. When introduced to a stranger, a Rottweiler will observe the person and respond with a wait-and-see attitude. Once he feels comfortable and not threatened by a newcomer, trust a Rottie to become a good-natured clown and, in time, to deliver some wet, sloppy kisses.

A well-trained, stable Rottweiler serves as an excellent ambassador for the breed. Once people have lived with a good Rottweiler, they seldom choose another breed the next time around.

HOME REQUIREMENTS

You don't need to live on a cattle ranch to own a Rottweiler, although what dog wouldn't love to spend his days exploring and running free-range and his evenings

Whatever the size of your property, a Rottie needs room to run.

relaxing in the home with you? A big working dog such as a Rottweiler does need a home with room to roam. As mentioned, a Rottie can weigh around 100 pounds; large males can weigh even more. Cramped quarters become even smaller once you add a dog of this size. There's also the herding factor to consider. Accustomed to working cattle, a Rottweiler can unintentionally nudge you into the wall without meaning to cause harm. It's just his way.

A Rottie pup or adolescent needs a good-sized fenced yard to accommodate his exercise requirements and to facilitate house-training. For an adult Rottweiler, a yard comes in handy in between formal activity sessions as a place to expend some excess energy, stretch his legs, or keep tabs on the property. A safe, enclosed space is ideal for ball-retrieving games or just relaxing. Spending some time in the fresh air also helps reduce boredom, which prevents destructive behavior indoors.

Your dog should never be left alone for long periods, no matter how secure or ideal the space may seem. There's no such thing as an "outside dog." All dogs, especially Rottweilers, are companion animals, and they crave human affection and attention. Rotties have an inherent need to be with and protect the ones they love. When they're relegated to a yard day in and day out, they become noisy, destructive, and aggressive. If your dog is hyperactive in the house or isn't house-trained, take the time to exercise him and train him. A Rottie is smart and will learn how to behave properly when given the opportunity.

When you own a large-breed dog, you should forget about maintaining a beautifully landscaped yard with manicured grass and flowers. Rottweilers are active, and they need a place to run and play, and they may even indulge in a little digging.

A fence that stands at least 6 feet high is a must, as Rotties can easily jump or climb over anything lower. Putting down a layer of cement beneath the fence line helps deter Rotties from using their paws to dig out underneath. Gates should have secure locks that prevent your dog from learning how to open them. If a Rottie wants to get out of the yard badly enough, he'll try and figure out a way to do it, so you must make your yard as escape-proof as possible. If you're using an outdoor fenced dog run, add an enclosed top.

When choosing a fence, avoid chain-link, as a Rottie can easily figure out how to hook his back feet into the links and climb up and over the fence and out of the yard. Choosing a privacy fence made from a solid material, such as wood or vinyl, helps prevent strangers from peering into your yard and teasing your dog. Blocking your dog's view also discourages territorial aggression.

Never opt for electronic fencing. For a Rottweiler, this system means disaster, as it won't keep people or animals from wandering onto your property, and will likely be ineffective at keeping your Rottie contained. If another dog or a person walks into the yard, your dog won't hesitate to chase the intruder back through the boundary and out of yard, despite the pain of electric shock.

A Rottweiler, or any dog for that matter, should never be chained up outside or left unattended on a tie-out cable. This is cruel punishment that is outlawed by many communities.

Expect your Rottie to keep a close eye on your property's perimeter. Although this trait varies to some degree within the breed, most Rotties have maintained their strong territorial instinct. The Rottweiler's heritage as a herding dog, keeping cattle inside a safe area and keeping intruders away, translates today into a desire to defend his owner's home, car, and property. If someone comes to visit while your dog is in the yard, and the person decides to use the back door instead of the front door, he may encounter a less-than-welcoming Rottweiler. To drive an ornery steer back to the herd, the Rotties used

Did You Know?

The Rottweiler's base coat color is black with rust to mahogany markings. Any other color is a disqualification in the show ring, according to the breed standards of major purebred registries, including the American Kennel Club and United Kennel Club. Red Rottweilers carry a higher incidence of cardiac problems and may have lighter colored eyes, which may develop problems. Reputable breeders do not intentionally breed for unusual colors.

The perfect Rottweiler owner is someone who has owned the breed before and knows to treat the dog as part of the family. Establishing strict boundaries from the first day that the dog comes home and providing early training and socialization are absolute musts.

— Sue Larsen, breeder of Falcon Crest Rottweilers in Newport, Rhode Island

If small dogs and rodents overly excite your Rottie during outdoor exercise, avoid areas where they are present. If that's not possible, do some training to help him ignore small creatures. Take food treats along, and when your Rottie sees another animal, ask your dog to sit and focus on you instead. When he complies, give him a treat. Eventually, he'll associate small prey with a reward instead of a conquest.

intimidation and sheer body strength to force the issue.

Before your Rottie goes out to exercise, always check the weather. Brisk, cold, or wet weather doesn't present a problem, but Rottweilers do not tolerate hot temperatures, as their black coat heats up quickly. If the temperature climbs to 75 degrees Fahrenheit or higher, a Rottie can easily suffer from heat stroke if he's exercising or in the direct sunlight for too long. Schedule your exercise and training sessions during early morning or evening hours, when it's cooler.

If you notice your Rottie panting heavily or showing signs of fatigue, give him some rest and try to cool him down. Either place a wet towel on the ground and let him stand on it (he'll cool off through the pads of his feet) or take him to a shady area and give him some water to drink.

LIVING WITH CHILDREN

In 1984, author and artist Alexandra Day was browsing in a Zurich bookshop when she came across a nineteenth-century cartoon about a Poodle left alone with an infant. The drawing inspired her to create a series of picture books, which became best sellers, about a Rottweiler named Carl who gently babysits an infant. While Day's paintings are attractive and present a saintlike portrayal of a Rottweiler, the general concept of a dog overseeing a child's needs is pure fiction. No canine, no matter how cute or mild-mannered, should ever be put in the role of caretaker or be left unsupervised with a child.

The Rottweiler has a strong instinct to pursue and capture prey, which around the house includes cats, small dogs, and children. For this reason, many Rottweiler breeders do not recommend that families with children younger than five or six years of age own this breed. Other people say that Rotties are good with younger children but must be raised with them from puppyhood.

If you already have an adult Rottweiler and are having a baby, socialize your dog with the small-fry world as often as possible. As you prepare the baby's room, give your dog plenty of opportunities to sniff the furniture, clothing, and supplies so that he has a chance to become accustomed to these new items before the baby arrives. Carry a doll around in your arms as if it were a baby. Talking and fussing over the doll lets the dog experience your new body language before the real baby comes home.

Invite friends with infants over to visit. This gives your Rottie the opportunity to become accustomed to the sights, smells, and sounds of babies. If possible, take your dog out walking where he can see and hear children.

Stock up on some new toys for your dog and dole them out as distractions when the baby comes home. This rewards

With proper instruction and supervision, children and Rotties can be the best of friends.

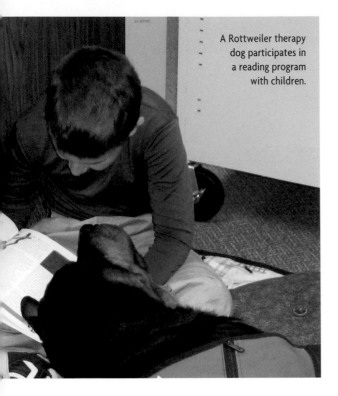

A Rottweiler therapy dog participates in a reading program with children.

Taking the baby out for a walk around the neighborhood? If you can handle both of them, bring your Rottie along, too. Never leave your child alone with your dog, regardless how sweet or well trained your dog is. An infant's odd noises and jerky movements may startle your dog and prompt him to act out in self-defense.

As your child grows, it's your responsibility to teach him or her to respect your Rottie's space and how to act around the dog. For their safety, children should never be allowed to run and scream in the house or yard when the dog is in the same area. The dog's strong prey instinct will kick in, and this incites him to chase after and pounce on your child.

Never let your toddler walk around the house carrying food. Your dog will think that your child is a walking meal ticket and will gobble up the goody, not realizing that small fingers are holding it. Insist that your child always eat snacks and meals at a table, out of your Rottie's reach.

Instruct your child that the Rottie's toys are off limits, as your dog will want them back and may bite a hand in the process. For the same reason, children should never grab anything away from the dog. Teach children that they should never pinch or pull the dog's skin or face or poke at his ears or eyes.

your dog and lets him associate the new addition to the family with positive experiences. Introduce your Rottweiler to the baby as a new member of the household pack by letting your dog sniff the baby. Don't worry; he's not going to give your infant any canine diseases, even if he gives the baby a little lick. Keeping your dog from meeting your baby gives the dog the impression that this newcomer is an intruder, and the dog may react as if he needs to protect the family.

Organize your schedule so that you can spend the same amount of time with your Rottweiler as you did before the baby arrived. Your dog shouldn't have to lose your attention, and he won't understand why you are neglecting him. A dog who is ignored once a baby arrives often resorts to destructive behavior as a way to get your attention.

NEEDY/INDEPENDENT TRAITS

Despite their initial aloofness with strangers, Rotties are entirely devoted to their families and need to stay close to them at all times. If you're in the bedroom and decide to walk to another room, expect a large black-and-rust partner to accompany you. It doesn't mater whether you're answering the door or getting a snack from the fridge. Your Rottie doesn't want

Gentle Dodger

Pamela Grant of Plano, Illinois, waited patiently at the airport's cargo area while her Rottie, Am./Can. Ch. Quail Ridge's Artful Dodger CGC, TT, TDI ("Dodger") catnapped on the floor at her feet. The pair was flying to a dog show, and Dodger was catching a few winks before the time came to hop into his pet carrier. Suddenly, Grant spotted a small toddler running down the hall in their direction.

"Doggie, doggie," the little girl called while rushing toward the 110-pound dog. Unfortunately, her parents were too far behind to intercept the child before she would reach the dog.

"I could hear the collective gasps of everyone in line, who probably thought that Dodger was going to jump up and maul the little girl,"

says Grant, a former president of the American Rottweiler Club. They needn't have worried. Grant had taken Dodger to training classes, had begun socializing her Rottie to people of all ages when he was a puppy, and knew that he was good with children. "Still, we had never been to an airport before. It was hectic and noisy, and I didn't want the girl to run up and scare him," Grant says.

Rather than wait to see what would happen, the owner took the initiative by waking up the big dog: "Dodger, who's coming to see you?" He picked his head up to look and laid it back down again. "The child ran up and laid her head on his big, thick neck and wide shoulders and hugged him so tightly," Grant says. "Dodger didn't even move a muscle, and I was so proud of him."

to miss a chance to stick like glue to your side. Test this out by walking into a room of the house and closing the door, leaving your dog on the other side. Open it a few minutes later, and he'll greet you with a silly grin and an enthusiastic wiggle as if you've been gone for days.

For people who live in a small home or who are constantly bustling around the house, it may present a problem to have a large dog who's always underfoot. This is not a huge issue, but one to take into consideration if you're thinking about getting this breed.

THE ROTTIE RUNDOWN

This working dog has it all!

COUNTRY OF ORIGIN: Germany

WHAT HIS FRIENDS CALL HIM: Rottie

SIZE: Males: 24 to 27 inches; females: 22 to 25 inches

OVERALL APPEARANCE: Medium to large, with the impression of strength and power; males appear more massive than females

COAT: Straight, coarse, thick, medium length

COLOR: Black with rust to mahogany markings

PERSONALITY TRAITS: Aloof, bossy, calm, courageous, intelligent, loyal, quiet, self-confident, willful

WITH KIDS: A strong chase instinct requires adult supervision at all times; early training around kids is strongly recommended

WITH OTHER ANIMALS: Good when raised with them from puppyhood; new pets should be introduced slowly and with caution

ENERGY LEVEL: Moderate; Rotties can become bored and overweight without enough exercise

GROOMING NEEDS: Regular brushing, especially during twice-annual shedding times; bathing and nail clipping as needed; daily tooth brushing

TRAINABILITY: Intelligent and eager to please, Rotties catch on quickly and don't appreciate long, repetitious practice sessions

LIVING ENVIRONMENT: Fenced yard, but shouldn't be left alone outdoors for long hours; needs to spend time indoors with owners and sleep inside

LIFESPAN: Average 10 to 12 years

A WORKING

ook into a Rottweiler's deep brown eyes, and you can imagine the scenes his ancestors witnessed 2,000 years ago. Serving as rugged war dogs, drover dogs, draft dogs, and farm dogs throughout its history, the breed was first developed from a Mastiff–type dog, or Molossian, bred to fight lions for Roman sport and to accompany soldiers.

It's no wonder that today's Rottweiler is calm, confident, and courageous, with a steadfast devotion to home and family. The Rottie of this generation doesn't fight wild game, but rather enjoys jogging, swimming, hiking, and participating in competitive activities with the people he loves. To better understand this powerful and loyal breed, it's important to see how the Rottweiler evolved.

ORIGINS AND ESTABLISHMENT

On a quest to conquer all of Europe around 50 BC, the Roman army brought along

The first American Rottweiler litter was born to Zilly v.d. Steinlach in 1930 and registered to the Allgemeiner Deutscher Rottweiler Klub (ADRK), the official breed club in Germany. The first AKC-registered Rottweiler was Stina vom Felsenmeer in 1931, and she whelped the first AKC-registered Rottweiler litter in the same year.

it's a
Fact

Before moving into a new community or renting a home with your Rottweiler, check the local laws. Some communities have breed-specific legislation that bans certain breeds, the Rottweiler included, claiming that they are too aggressive. Although your dog may have a good temperament and be well trained, this type of legislation does not make provisions for individual dogs.

intelligent gladiator dogs to drive and protect their food source—herds of cattle that helped feed the soldiers. As the Romans marched north and followed Alpine passes along the Neckar River in southwestern Germany, they took over the 2,000-year-old town of Arae Flaviae in approximately AD 74. The Romans transformed it into an important administrative center, complete with a Roman bath and red-tile roofing on the buildings. Eventually, the cultural center became known by the German name Rottwil ("red villa") and later Rottweil.

Over centuries, Rottweil became the center of commerce, and cattlemen used the descendants of the Roman canines as all-around cattle dogs. During the Middle Ages, these dogs closely resembled the modern Rottweiler. From herding in the butcher's yard to carting the slaughtered meat around town and driving cattle from town to town, the dogs were vital working companions. After delivering a herd to market for sale, the Rottweiler protected the drover as he walked home with a purse full of money; in fact, the dog often had the purse tied around his neck to deter robbers.

The Rottweiler, or *Rottweil metzger-hund*, was known as the butcher's dog and was often crossed with neighboring breeds, such as the Greater Swiss Mountain Dog, the Bernese Mountain Dog, the Entlebucher, and the Appenzeller. The dogs were also bred to fighting breeds that were used to hunt wild game.

Later, donkeys and then the railroad replaced the need for the Rottweiler's herding and carting abilities, and the dogs' population declined. As the story goes, by 1900, only one Rottweiler lived in the town, but fanciers became interested in preserving the breed. Using remaining dogs scattered throughout Europe and breeding to perpetuate the best attributes, German breeders revived the Rottweiler.

In 1883, fancier Albert Kull wrote the first breed standard, which established a description of the characteristics that the ideal Rottweiler should possess, both physically and temperamentally. While today's Rottweiler is a black and tan dog without any white markings, Kull's standard permitted black stripes on an ash-gray background with yellow markings, plain red with a black nose, or dark wolf gray with a black head and saddle, but always with yellow markings, and a few white markings were permissible.

By 1910, the German Police Dog Association had officially recognized Rottweilers as police dogs alongside the German Shepherd Dog, the Doberman Pinscher, and the Airedale Terrier, and the officers valued them because of their protective, intelligent, and stable nature. The Allgemeiner Deutscher Rottweiler Klub (ADRK), which translates to "General German Rottweiler Club," was formed in 1921, and still exists as the official breed club in Germany. At the time, the club controlled the breed and changed the coat requirements to black with clearly defined

 In most countries other than the United States, the Rottweiler has an undocked tail.

We have the Europeans to thank for placing character high on the Rottweiler's priority list. Today, the breed is still wonderfully calm, confident, and courageous and has maintained his herding and guarding instincts.

—Catherine M. Thompson, a Rottweiler breeder and the ARC obedience chairperson from Washington Court House, Ohio

mahogany to yellow markings; small white markings on the chest and belly were undesirable. The club required Rottweilers to prove their expertise as working dogs before they could receive their German championships.

ARRIVAL IN AMERICA

The Rottweiler moved on to new challenges when German immigrants brought the breed to the United States in the 1920s. The first litter was whelped in 1930 and was registered with the ADRK in Germany, as the American Kennel Club (AKC) did not recognize the breed at that time.

When any new breed first appears, people unfamiliar with it tend to think of it as a mixed breed. Rottweilers endured the same criticism and were ignored by serious dog-show fanciers. However, because breeding requirements in the United States were far less restrictive than those of the ADRK, the Rottweiler's numbers increased, and the breed became established in America in a fairly short time due to the efforts of several dedicated kennels. These kennels included Rodsden, Follow Me, Palos Park, Von Stahl, Srigo, Freeger, Panamint, Wellwood, Crestwood, Giralda, and Hohenreissach, all of which helped build the breed's foundation in the United States and can be found behind most American Rottweilers today.

In 1931, the AKC began to record Rottweilers in its stud book, and the breed was recognized as part of its Working Group. In 1940, the AKC registered eleven Rottweilers. The AKC breed standard, originally published in 1935, was revised in 1971 and again in 1990. The American Rottweiler Club (ARC) was formed in 1973 and became a member club of the AKC in 1991; the ARC is the AKC national parent club for the breed.

The AKC registered only seventy-seven Rottweilers in 1960, and the breed was considered rare in the United States until the 1970s and 1980s. However, as more and more people began to look for a dog for protection, the breed's popularity as a handsome, macho canine status symbol began to soar.

By the mid-1990s, the AKC was registering more than 100,000 Rottweilers each year, ranking it as the second most popular breed in the United States during this time. While responsible, ethical breeders worked to preserve the Rotttweiler's health, temperament, conformation, and natural abilities, the breed's explosion in popularity brought with it unscrupulous breeders who produced puppies for the sole purpose of making some quick cash. These people paid little attention to which males they paired with which females and what the matings would produce in terms of health, temperament, and conformation, and, as a result, the overall quality of the breed diminished. Unstable, unhealthy Rotties began to appear, and the breed developed a bad reputation as an aggressive biter. By 1999, the breed's ranking had dropped to eighth in popularity; in 2010, it was eleventh.

BREED STANDARD

The difference between having a stable, confident, and courageous dog and an aggressive menace has everything to do with the breed standard. The details in the Rottweiler standard describe an athletic dog with a purpose and all of the traits he must have to perform the job he was originally bred to do. When you have a Rottie who conforms to the standard, and you provide him with early socialization and positive training, you have the foundation for a dog who represents what the breed was meant to be.

In terms of physical characteristics, the Rottie's powerful build must be compact but never so heavy that he's not quick and agile enough to round up and herd cattle. His head should be broad between the ears with few wrinkles, giving a powerful appearance.

The eyes should be deep brown and almond shaped, exuding self-confidence and courage. From his days herding cattle, the Rottweiler needed to stand his ground and subdue an awkward cow or bull that challenged him. He used his eyes to give the animal a hard look, which convinced it to back down. The AKC breed standard requires the Rottweiler's tail to be docked short, close to the body, leaving one or two tail vertebrae. Breeders have tail docking performed in very young puppies. Historically, tails were docked to prevent them from getting tangled in the cart and sustaining other types of damage. In Europe, docking is banned, and the tail grows naturally and resembles the Labrador Retriever's "otter" tail.

Written by members of the American Rottweiler Club and approved by the AKC, the breed standard is a blueprint for the ideal Rottweiler. Whether you want to show your dog or just want to live with a wonderful pet, your Rottweiler should come as close as possible to the standard—it's a description that defines his utility as a working guardian and his unique set of characteristics.

It's the breed standard that keeps the breed looking and acting the same way for generations and preserves those hallmark

Did You Know?

Every year, the American Rottweiler Club presents Anvil TRUE Awards to outstanding Rottweilers in recognition of service performed. Owners and their Rottweilers are eligible if they spend a minimum of twenty-five hours a year donating their time in nursing homes, hospitals, search and rescue, law enforcement, or educating the public by visiting schools and information booths.

SMART TIP!

Keep a record of your Rottie's life by taking photographs of him every year on his birthday or the day you adopted him. Jot down notes about his health, activity level, sleep patterns, what he likes to eat, and funny things he does. This documents his special time with you and can even help you pinpoint changes that could indicate a health problem.

qualities that were important to those who established the breed. While styles in fashion and automobiles and other trends change from time to time, the correctly bred Rottweiler will never change.

EXCEPTIONAL EXAMPLES

Many Rottweilers serve their owners every day with pride and panache, but a few belong to the ranks of distinguished award winners.

Sheer Faith

The AKC presents its Humane Fund Awards for Canine Excellence, or ACEs, to exemplary dogs who have significantly benefited a community or an individual. The first awards were given in 2000, and one dog is awarded annually in each of five categories: law enforcement, search and rescue, therapy, service, and exemplary companion.

In 2005, Leana Beasley's dog, Faith, was the first Rottweiler to receive an ACE. Faith is a highly skilled certified service dog in seizure, respiratory, and cardiac alert and response; mobility assistance; emergency water rescue; and cart pulling. Trained by the Assistance Dog Club of Puget Sound, Washington, Faith understands more than 150 commands that help Beasley in her day-to-day tasks.

One day, Faith realized that something was wrong with Beasley and tried to alert her owner. Sitting in her wheelchair, Beasley didn't realize that she was having a toxic reaction to a new medication, and she fell to the floor and began having seizures. Realizing that commands were useless, Faith assessed the situation and saved Beasley's life. The dog took the phone off the hook, pushed the special 9-1-1 speed-dial button, and barked into the phone. She returned to Beasley and, using her seizure response training, rolled her owner into a recovery position. When help arrived, Faith recognized a police uniform and unlocked the door. The American Red Cross presented Faith with its Real Hero Award, making her the first nonhuman recipient.

Rumor's Story

When breeder Steph Anderson of South Sioux City, Nebraska, learned that owners were neglecting a Rottie who she had

it's a Fact

In 1939, Gero V. Rabenhorst became the first Rottweiler to earn an AKC Companion Dog (CD) title, a Companion Dog Excellent (CDX) title in 1940, and the first Utility Dog (UD) title in 1941. Millsap's Lamgrave Salem Von Brabant UDTX earned the breed's first Novice Agility title in 1994.

NOTABLE & QUOTABLE

This breed has a long history of service and loyalty to its owners, and the Rottweiler is a big, energetic dog with a great deal of power. He can easily learn how to listen and pay attention to you because his ancestors did exactly that.

—Jill Kessler, president of the Golden State Rottweiler Club and cofounder of Rottweiler Rescue of Los Angeles in Pacific Palisades, Calfornia

The Rottie's expression has melted many a heart.

Junior Showmanship, obedience, and rally, and the two became inseparable.

"You could see that Francisco was gaining self-confidence, and his overall demeanor just changed from sullen and quiet to outgoing and [interested in] making plans for the future," Anderson says.

In 2007, Rumor received the AKC's ACE in the exemplary companion dog category.

Turbo Hugs

People say that everything is big in Texas, and this seems especially true of Pat Crawford's Rottweiler, Turbo, who has an enormous heart of gold. In 2009, the three-year-old dog from Valley View, Texas, was inducted into the Texas Animal Hall of Fame for his therapy work with children, the elderly, and the disabled.

In 2007, Crawford and Turbo logged more than 400 hours of visits to the Pecan Tree Rehabilitation Center and the Wheeler House, both in Gainesville. By gently nudging and laying his head in the residents' laps, few could resist petting and hugging Turbo. The Rottweiler's visits have provided comfort to seriously ill patients, and he has offered encouragement to those in physical therapy.

With students at the Valley View Elementary School, Turbo helps Crawford demonstrate responsible pet ownership and pet safety. The big dog sits with students as they read, solve math problems, and vie for his attention.

This special Rottweiler is also a certified water dog and is capable of towing boats through the water and helping locate stranded swimmers. Turbo was honored with the American Rottweiler Club's prestigious Anvil TRUE Award for therapy work and was in the ARC's top ten for obedience in 2007.

previously sold to them, she stepped in to take the dog back. Rumor, a four-year-old female, arrived back with Anderson just in time. A foster parent, Anderson had just agreed to care for a teenage boy whose father had been sent to prison and whose mother had a drug problem.

"I took Francisco with me to pick up Rumor, and something magical happened between them when he put her into my car," Anderson says. "Francisco gave her so much love and attention, and the dog just glowed with excitement every time she saw him."

Prior to meeting one another, both boy and dog had been cold to those around them, but gradually they relaxed and began to interact with others. Francisco began showing Rumor in conformation,

You have an unbreakable bond with your dog, but do you always understand him? Go online and download "Dog Speak," which outlines how dogs communicate. Find out what your Rottweiler is saying when he barks, howls, or growls. Go to **DogChannel.com/ Club-Rottie** and click on "Downloads."

A Search and Rescue Angel

On a hot Sunday afternoon in July 2009, the family of eight-year-old Travis Covey became frantic when their little boy went outdoors to play and failed to return home in Smithville Lake, Missouri.

At 9 a.m. the next day, Heddie Leger received a call to bring her Rottweiler, Halo (Double D Full Circle V Hedron RN, CGC, RTD), to the scene. Halo's days of playing hide and seek as a puppy had paid off. Now a certified area search and rescue dog, Halo had also been trained to locate the scent of human decomposition and bodies underwater.

Leger and four-year-old Halo joined law-enforcement officials and three other dog-and-handler search teams. Before setting off to comb through separate quadrants of the wooded area, the dogs were given a few articles of the boy's clothing. Leger told her dog, "Halo, check scent!"

Halo sniffed the garments to catch the aroma, and she put her head down before moving it back up again. "Halo, find scent," Leger told her.

On most searches, Halo picks up the scent and quickly turns her head in the direction it's coming from. She follows the essence as it moves through the air, isolates it, and turns her head and body in that direction.

"I always know when Halo finds the exact scent ... her body goes erect, and she starts running in a wide semi-circle," says Leger. "Then she stops where the scent is the strongest, trots back to me, and returns to the location and alerts by sitting, as a bark could scare someone. She always has a big grin on her face, and her little tail wags a mile a minute."

Two hours later, the boy was found safe, but Halo couldn't claim the find. "Then the sheriff realized that he dropped his keys in the woods, and we headed out again to help him, despite the fact that people were skeptical that a dog could locate metal," Leger remembers.

Forty volunteers checked the woods for several hours, and this time the Rottweiler's talent proved victorious. "When I saw Halo sitting next to those keys on the ground, I praised her to bits and gave her a huge handful of hot dogs as a reward, but the sheriff presented her with a badge."

Today's Rottweiler puts his working ability to good use as a high-flying competitor, an active companion, and a loyal family member.

A ROTTIE

IN THE FAMILY

The decision to live with a powerful dog that can weigh around 100 pounds requires careful deliberation. While roly-poly Rottweiler puppies are hard to resist, they grow up and carry with them a decade or more of responsibility. Whether you acquire a puppy or adopt an adult, your Rottie will share your life as an active companion and will play an important role in your household routine. He'll reflect the care and affection you show him and represent your emotional investment.

Rotties require a sizable amount of your attention, and you'll need to spend time training and socializing your dog. This is a sensitive, intelligent, and loyal breed that wants to bond with you. A Rottie makes every effort to please his owners, but his owners in turn must provide for the dog's needs. Your Rottie is an active dog who needs a minimum of two walks plus structured exercise and playtime every day to keep his mind and body in good shape.

As mentioned, you'll need to securely enclose your yard with at least a 6-foot-

Only one type of Rottweiler is correct, regardless if the dog comes from German or American stock. Variations in size or in the shape of the body or head may occur in any breeding. The only difference is that Rottweilers born in Germany after 1999 cannot have docked tails.

it's a
Fact

high fence so that your Rottie won't escape. Then again, this isn't a breed that can be left alone for long hours in the yard. Trust a Rottweiler to cause a ruckus and become destructive if he feels isolated and lonely.

Don't underestimate how much space a Rottweiler takes up inside the house. While a Rottie puppy fits easily in most rooms of your home, by six months of age, your dog will likely weigh more than 70 pounds and bump into walls and furniture when simply turning around.

Plan on securing loose cords and putting away your prized possessions until you teach your Rottie the difference between his toys and your belongings. He's a bull in a china shop and can't help causing damage to furniture, walls, and floors. You'll need to dog-proof the house before your Rottie comes home so you don't have to worry if he starts chewing.

The decision to acquire a Rottweiler shouldn't be taken lightly, but once you've decided to take the plunge, your next step is locating the right Rottie for you.

PURCHASING A ROTTIE PUPPY

A Rottweiler pup adds enthusiasm and high energy to your home and reaffirms everything that is good and joyous in life. Simply interacting with your black and rust teddy bear is healthy, as scientists claim that playing with your puppy increases the feel-good hormones oxytocin and dopamine in your brain. The bonding experience also lowers stress and instills well-being.

This exhilaration will sustain you through the challenging and frustrating times that your new puppy can bring. It takes time and patience to figure out canine body language, and your dog must also learn to understand what you're trying to teach him. Selecting the right puppy—one who is healthy and stable—from a reputable breeder makes it so much easier for you to adapt to puppy and vice versa.

When you acquire a puppy, you have the opportunity to train him exactly the way you want. Seeing the pup's parents and other relatives on the breeder's premises provides a blueprint of your pup's eventual appearance and behavior, but the final choice is still up to you.

Questions for Owners and Breeders

A good breeder wants to know that each and every one of his or her pups is going to a suitable home with responsible, prepared owners. Don't be surprised if the breeder asks you a few questions.

Have you ever owned a Rottweiler? The breeder wants to know how familiar you are with the breed and if you understand the challenges of the breed's size and temperament. If you have never owned a Rottie, explain your history with other breeds and talk about what you know about Rottweilers.

Why do you want a Rottweiler? A Rottweiler is more than just a striking face and muscular body. The breed requires time and attention for training and socialization. The breeder wants to know that this is not an impulse purchase and that you've care-

Did You Know?

While pet-quality Rottweilers may have cosmetic faults that are not acceptable in the show ring, they can still compete in performance events. Having pet-quality conformation should not affect a dog's health or temperament.

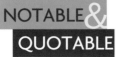

NOTABLE & QUOTABLE

When some people acquire a Rottweiler puppy, they under-estimate how big he'll grow. If they're unprepared to own a large, active breed, they can quickly become overwhelmed. It's one of the reasons many Rotties wind up in rescue.

— Jill Kessler, co-founder of Rottweiler Rescue of Los Angeles, California

fully considered what's involved in owning this breed. It's important that you appreciate the breed's personality and activity level and are prepared to make the commitment to raising a Rottie right.

How much time do you spend at home? Rotties aren't happy in the backyard alone all day; they thrive on human interaction.

Where do you plan to keep your dog when you're not home? A breeder wants to know that your dog will be safe in your absence.

Will you sign a contract agreeing not to breed your Rottweiler and to spay or neuter? The last thing reputable breeders want is to add to the pet overpopulation problem. Breeding should be left to knowledgeable breeders.

Are there children or small pets in the home? Rottweilers have a strong instinct to chase moving objects, and this includes children and small pets. Your Rottweiler will need early training to learn how to behave around children and other pets, and children must be taught how to behave around a large dog. You will always need to supervise their interaction.

Do you have the time to take your Rottweiler to training classes or to work **with a trainer?** If so, this reassures the breeder that you will learn how to provide firm leadership and that your dog will become a well-behaved member of your household and the community.

There are also questions that you should ask the breeder. A reputable breeder will not be put off by your questions, and in fact will expect them. Here are examples of what you should ask a breeder.

Are the parents of the puppies older than two? The parents should be mature and old enough to undergo health testing to prove that they do not have hip dysplasia. The results of hip dysplasia screening are not reliable until a dog has reached at least two years of age.

What health tests do you perform on your breeding stock and on the puppies, and may I see copies of the test results? Beware of a breeder who says that none of his or her dogs have health problems. Every breed has health issues, and they can crop up in any bloodline. A reputable breeder should not breed dogs who have not passed health screenings, and the breeder should be happy to show you copies of health certifications. Breeding stock must be certified free of hip and elbow dysplasia by the Orthopedic Foundation for Animals (OFA) based on X-ray evaluation of these joints. Studies show that breeding dogs with normal hips and elbows produces less incidence of joint disease.

A board-certified veterinary ophthalmologist should examine the eyes of dogs over the age of two, and breeding stock should be certified free of hereditary eye disease by the Canine Eye Registration Foundation (CERF). CERF registration is only good for twelve months, so breeders must have their dogs retested annually. Breeding dogs should also be examined by a veterinarian

Did You Know?

In a typical sales contract, a reputable breeder guarantees that a puppy is in good health at the time of the sale, and the buyer agrees to provide veterinary care, a healthy diet, safe housing, training, and grooming. The contract should also state if the puppy is being sold as a show prospect or as a pet.

Questions to Expect

Be prepared for the breeder to ask you some questions, too.

JOIN OUR
ONLINE
**Club
Rottie™**

1. Have you previously owned a Rottweiler?

The breeder is trying to gauge how familiar you are with the Rottie. If you have never owned one, illustrate your knowledge of the breed by telling the breeder about your research.

2. Do you have children? What are their ages?

Some breeders are wary about selling a puppy to families with younger children.

This isn't a steadfast rule, and some breeders insist on meeting the kids to see how they handle puppies. It all depends on the breeder.

3. How long have you wanted a Rottie?

This helps a breeder know if your purchase is an impulse buy or a carefully thought-out decision. Buying on impulse is one of the biggest mistakes owners can make. Be patient.

Join Club Rottie to get a complete list of questions that a breeder should ask you. Click on "Downloads" at **DogChannel.com/Club-Rottie.**

for the presence of subaortic stenosis, a heart defect.

Have your dogs had cruciate ligament injuries, von Willebrand's disease, hypothyroidism, or orthopedic disorders such as osteochondritis? Members of the American Rottweiler Club (ARC), the breed's parent club, are discouraged from breeding dogs with these (or any) disorders, which may have genetic components.

Do you belong to a Rottweiler club? When a breeder is a member of a national, regional, or local Rottweiler club, he or she agrees to abide by the club's code of ethics regarding breeding practices. This person is also connected to a network of other breeders who help each other stay current on topics such as the latest advances in behavior, care, health, and training.

Why did you breed this litter? You want the breeder to tell you that he or she hopes to produce better offspring than the parents or to improve the breed's health, temperament, and overall type.

How long have you bred Rottweilers? Look for a breeder with at least several years of experience. A track record shows dedication and an understanding of the breed. You want to acquire a puppy from someone who is willing and able to help you when you call with a question or a problem.

How many litters do you breed each year? Breeding a litter requires an abundance of time and patience and includes not only choosing the breeding pair, caring for a pregnant dam, and raising the puppies, but also screening buyers to ensure that each pup goes to a good home. Producing more than two litters per year signifies that a breeder is trying to make a profit rather than being concerned about the welfare of the puppies and the betterment of the breed.

What titles do your dogs have? If either the sire (father) or the dam (mother), or both, are show champions, it shows that the parents are quality dogs who meet the requirements of the breed standard. If they've earned Canine Good Citizen certification or possess obedience or performance titles, it indicates that the breeder spends time training his or her dogs and is actively involved in the world of dog sports.

What is your health guarantee and sales policy? A reputable breeder should offer a refund or a new puppy if your pup develops an unforeseen health problem within a certain time frame. A reputable breeder also will always take a dog back at any time, regardless of why you can no longer care for him.

Evaluating Breeders

Resist the urge to buy a puppy from the first breeder you encounter. Take some time to interview breeders and locate one with quality puppies and with whom you feel comfortable. You're going to have this dog for many years, so spending a few weeks or months early on to find the right breeder and the right puppy definitely pays off.

Your best source for a Rottweiler puppy is a conscientious breeder with an outstanding reputation and qualifications. This is far more important than if the breeder lives close by, if the puppy is less expensive than you expected, or if puppies are available right away. A day's drive is nothing if it means that you'll spend the next ten or more years with a healthy, sound, well-adjusted Rottweiler who is a good example of his breed.

The best breeder is passionate about the dogs he or she produces, how they are raised, and the homes that they go to. Buy a puppy from someone who shows his or

Two Special Rotties

When Steven and Jami Nytko visited Rottweiler Rescue of Los Angeles (RRLA), they found Jäger, a two-and-a-half-year-old male who had been brought to the rescue six months prior. "Although we wanted a female, he reminded us of the two Labrador Retrievers we had recently lost, and we couldn't stop thinking about him," Steven says. "Later, we learned that he had spent his life living in the backyard and was never socialized because he urinated in the house and was too dominant for [his owners] to manage."

The Nytkos began with basic obedience training, but it took six months for Jäger's true personality to emerge. "Strangers would think he was friendly, but if they came too close, he would jump and bark or growl," Steven says. "He never did this with us, but it was a huge problem with everyone else."

Even a simple walk on the street proved exhausting, recalls Steven. "Noisy vehicles sent him into a frenzy, and he went after anything that moved."

Some trainers and well-meaning friends told the Nytkos that they would never "fix" their Rottie's rotten behavior. Help came after Jami interviewed a long list of professional trainers and chose one who specialized in dogs with aggressive behavior. The Nytkos spent six weeks working with the trainer to desensitize Jäger to social interactions with people.

"He's a dominant dog, and we had to teach him how to stop acting badly," Steven says. "We also had to be selective in who we let pet our dog because people who were afraid would set him off."

Training classes three days a week, trips to crowded parking lots, and plenty of patience helped transform Jäger into a well-behaved, reliable Rottweiler. Within seven months, he earned AKC titles in obedience (Companion Dog), rally (Rally Advanced Excellent), and tracking (Tracking Dog), as well as his Canine Good Citizen (CGC) certification.

"Once we dealt with his basic issues, we discovered that he had an excellent work ethic," Steven says. "The first time we attached him to a cart, he was so excited." In no time, Jäger obtained the American Rottweiler Club's Carting Intermediate (CI) and Carting Team Started (CST) titles.

As Jäger settled into a routine, the Nytkos' desire to add a female Rottweiler to the household became even stronger. They returned to RRLA and adopted shy Bella, abandoned a year earlier by an owner who didn't want to repair her torn cruciate ligament. Newly christened as Cold Stone's Trulee Scrumptious ("Trulee"), she took to Jäger right away, and the two became fast friends.

her dogs, as this person is knowledgeable about the breed standard and is dedicated to producing the best possible Rottweiler puppies—puppies who look and act the way the breed was originally intended. Not every pup in a show-bred litter will make it to the show ring, but the pet-quality puppies in that litter are raised as if they are going to be future champions.

Look for a breeder who belongs to the breed's parent club. ARC members agree to abide by mandatory breeding practices established by the organization, which helps encourage and promote quality breeding. These practices include breeding to the breed standard, carefully planning all litters, and only breeding dogs who have the necessary health clearances. Member breeders sell all dogs with a written contract, offer a health guarantee, require that all pet-quality pups be spayed or neutered, and have a lifetime responsibility for all of the puppies they produce.

If a breeder tries to sell you a puppy of a rare color or that is much smaller or larger than specified in the breed standard, run the other way. These qualities should not be considered unique or desirable. Plus, no breeder can foresee exactly how large a puppy will be when he grows up, so an oversized puppy that the breeder promises will grow up to be extra-large may very well end up average-sized.

How to Select a Puppy

Once you've chosen a good breeder, the next step is to choose your puppy once a litter is available. Selecting a healthy Rottie puppy is your first priority. The breeder will invite you to come and observe the litter a few weeks before the pups are ready to go to their new homes. Start by watching the pups in their play area. The surroundings should be clean and well lit with a variety of interesting toys and a clean bowl of water. The pups should exude fitness, vigor, and well-being. Healthy pups appear active, friendly, and playful—jumping up on you, bringing you toys, and wrestling with their littermates.

Look for these signs of good health:

- Clear eyes that aren't red or runny
- No discharge coming from the nose
- Dry, odorless ears (a musty odor signals an infection)
- Healthy skin and coat without any skin irritations or bald spots; the pup should not be scratching excessively or biting at his skin, which may indicate fleas (fleas can be seen as little black specks on the abdomen or at the base of the tail)
- Smooth, easy, energetic movement with no limping
- Normal weight and body condition; the abdomen should not appear distended
- Normal stools without bloody discharge or signs of diarrhea

Before visiting a breeder and picking a puppy, decide on the goals you'd like to pursue with your Rottie in the future. If you're interested in showing your dog in conformation and the breeder will allow you to buy a show-quality puppy, the breeder will help you choose the best show prospect. For a great pet, choose a pup with a middle-of-the road demeanor, rather than the most outgoing or quietest pup in the litter. If you have visions of competing in dog sports with your Rottie, the breeder can help you choose a motivated pup with drive and a desire to please.

Choosing a puppy from a responsible breeder gives you the advantage of seeing the pup's parents and other relatives and gives you some idea of what your pup will

With one Rottie puppy cuter than the next, it's hard not to choose a pup based on looks alone; however, much more than that must factor into your decision.

Breeder Q&A

Here are some questions you should ask a breeder and the answers you want.

Q. How often do you have litters available?

A. You want to hear "once or twice a year" or "occasionally" because a breeder who doesn't have litters that often is probably more concerned with the quality of his or her puppies than with making money.

Q. What kinds of health problems do Rotties have?

A. Beware of a breeder who says "none." In Rottweilers, health problems include anterior cruciate ligament rupture, various eye diseases, and subvalvular aortic stenosis, a heart defect.

Get a complete list of questions to ask an Rottie breeder—and the ideal answers—at Club Rottie. Log onto **DogChannel.com/Club-Rottie** and click on "Downloads."

grow up to look and act like. If you don't like the parents, don't buy the puppy.

A reputable breeder will keep the puppies until they are between eight and twelve weeks old. Until then, the pups need to bond with their mother and each other. Acquiring a puppy after twelve weeks is acceptable as long as he receives lots of human contact and is well socialized.

Often a breeder will hold on to a show prospect but will place the dog in a pet home months later if the dog fails to reach his show potential or develops a disqualifying fault, such as an incorrect bite, a coat that's too long, or a lack of proper markings. Acquiring an older puppy who is house-trained, leash-trained, and beyond the chewing stage is often a bonus.

Think twice before buying a shy or lethargic pup or one who cowers, as these traits could indicate temperament issues that you may not be equipped to take on. Instead, choose a healthy, well-adjusted puppy who is happy-go-lucky and eager to approach you.

Temperament Tests

A breeder watches his or her puppies play and interact with each other every day from the day the litter is born. Experienced Rottweiler breeders know their puppies better than a prospective buyer ever could from just one or two visits. When sizing up a puppy's temperament, trust the breeder's judgment. Ask the breeder to help you choose a puppy with the personality and energy level that best matches your family and lifestyle, as Rottweiler pups can range from laid-back to busybody.

A good family companion may be the puppy who prefers to watch and wait for attention rather than the puppy who always pushes to the front to be where the action is. A dominant dog makes a great competitor but is probably not the best choice for a relaxed household.

Many breeders use temperament, or puppy aptitude, tests to assess a pup's responses to certain situations and stimuli. Designed by experts in canine behavior, the tests may identify certain personality traits, but opinions differ about the tests' accuracy. A puppy's results may differ if the test is repeated a second, third, or even a fourth time. Every test is a learning experience for the puppy, which will affect the response.

Temperament tests are usually administered to puppies between seven and ten weeks of age and include a few basics to determine level of dominance, trainability, and interest in people. Exercises include cradling the pup on his back while holding him gently on the chest to indicate his level of independence, suspending the pup under his armpits with his legs dangling to show willfulness, banging a loud pan to test the pup's noise sensitivity, and calling the pup from a distance to show the pup's interest in companionship.

No test is a complete predictor of what a pup's behavior will be like once he goes to a new home. Many personality traits, such as aggression, territorial vocalization,

it's a
Fact

According to the breed standard, Rottie males range in size from 22 to 27 inches tall at the shoulder, while females should measure 22 to 25 inches. In both sexes, the mid-range is preferable. The correct proportion of height to length of 9 to 10 is most important.

excessive reactivity, and many forms of fear, don't emerge until maturity. Some traits are not solely genetic and may be learned. Environment and training play an integral role in behavior.

Papers from the Breeder

Discuss all terms of the sale with your breeder before purchasing your puppy. The breeder should give you a packet of papers confirming the agreement for the puppy you select. Conscientious breeders often prepare puppy-care information for new owners. Take the time to read everything, and if there's anything that you're not sure about, ask the breeder to explain it.

Sales agreement: This document confirms the conditions of the purchase and should include the purchase price, the terms of the breeder's health guarantee, the spay/neuter requirement for a pet-quality dog, and the breeder's promise to take the dog back if you can no longer care for him.

Pedigree: The breeder should provide a three-, four- or five-generation pedigree, or family tree, that lists all of the puppies' ancestors. Look for initials before or after the dogs' names; these indicate champion or performance titles.

Registration papers: When both the sire and dam of the litter are registered with a purebred registry, such as the American Kennel Club or the United Kennel Club, the breeder can apply to register the puppies. The breeder should give you a registration application when you take the puppy home so that you can register the pup in your name. Be wary if the breeder promises to send you the registration papers later; you should take them home with your puppy.

Health records: You should receive documentation of the puppy's date of birth, any immunizations and wormings given, the results of veterinary examinations, and copies of any health clearances. Show all of this paperwork to your veterinarian when you take the puppy in for his first visit, which you should schedule for a day or two after you bring him home.

Care instructions: Instructions should include what kind of food and how much to feed your Rottweiler at different life stages, exercise requirements, advice on grooming, and recommendations on training and socialization.

ADOPTING FROM A SHELTER OR RESCUE

If the thought of giving a deserving adult Rottweiler a second chance rather than adding a puppy to your home appeals to

Many adult Rottweilers are in the care of breed rescue groups as they await second chances in loving homes.

you, contact Rottweiler rescue, where you'll encounter an unexpected gift wrapped in black and rust fur. Considered an adult at one year of age and fully mature by age three, the full-grown Rottweiler you adopt still has a lot of puppy antics left. Both males and females will assume the goofy adolescent role despite their actual age.

Adopting an adult Rottweiler gives you the advantage of knowing exactly how large your dog will be when full-grown. The adult Rottie may already have been spayed or neutered, may be house-trained, and may know some basic obedience skills, but much of the dog's background and previous training will be a mystery.

Reputable Rottweiler rescue groups often use temperament tests to gauge their dogs' personalities before matching them up with new owners. The American Temperament Test Society (www.atts.org) provides evaluation guidelines for dogs of at least eighteen months of age to measure various aspects of temperament, including stability, shyness, aggressiveness, friendliness, and instinct for protectiveness. Also, most rescue groups house their adoptees with volunteer foster families who have experience with the breed, so the volunteers get to learn a lot about the dogs in a home environment.

Purebred Rotties also end up for adoption in animal shelters. Many shelters use the ASPCA's Meet Your Match SAFER (Safety Assessment For Evaluating Rehoming) program or the ADOPT (Assess Dogs on Practical Tasks) protocol to assess possible future aggression. Ask adoption coordinators at the shelter for the results of these tests as well as for their own observations of any dog you're considering.

The American Rottweiler Club offers rescue support and information through the Rottweiler Rescue Foundation (www.rottnet. net). You can also check North East Rottweiler Rescue & Referral's website (www.rottrescue.org) for a list of Rottweiler rescue groups throughout the United States.

Healthy Puppy Signs

Here are a few things you should look for when selecting a puppy from a litter.

1. **NOSE:** It should be slightly moist to the touch, but there shouldn't be excessive discharge. The puppy should not be sneezing or sniffling persistently.

2. **SKIN AND COAT:** Your Rottie puppy's coat should be soft and shiny, without flakes or excessive shedding. Watch out for patches of missing hair, redness, bumps, or sores. The pup should have a pleasant smell. Check for parasites, such as fleas or ticks.

3. **BEHAVIOR:** A healthy Rottie puppy may be sleepy, but he should not be lethargic. A healthy puppy will be playful at times, not isolated in a corner. You should see occasional bursts of energy and interaction with his littermates. When it's mealtime, a healthy puppy will take an interest in his food.

There are other signs to look for when picking out the perfect Rottie puppy for your lifestyle. Download the list at **DogChannel.com/Club-Rottie.**

NOTABLE & QUOTABLE

When you're buying a purebred puppy, you're really buying the breeder's expertise, too. It's the serious breeders who are ready, willing, and able to help you for the life of the dog, not just until the check clears. They're also willing to take the puppy back if you're unable to keep the dog.

—Daisy Okas, former assistant vice president of communications for the American Kennel Club in New York, New York

CHAPTER
4

READY FOR

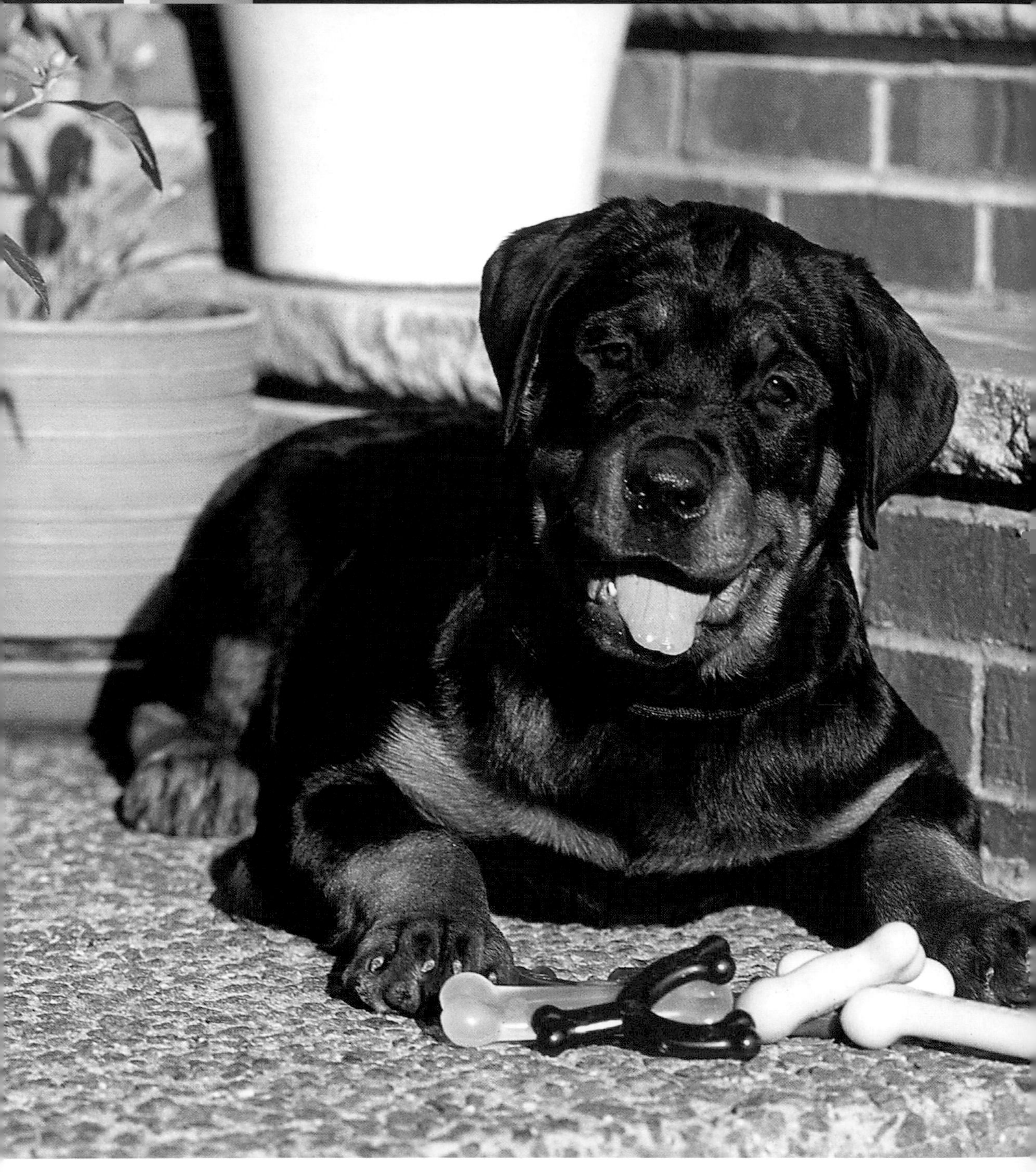

N ow that you've researched your breed, found a great breeder, and picked out the perfect Rottweiler puppy, you might have to wait a few weeks until the pup is old enough to leave his mother and siblings. That's OK. The delay gives you time to prepare the household for the arrival of big puppy paws. The puppy-proofing advice in this chapter goes for adopted adult dogs, too. No matter the age of your new Rottie addition, make sure that your home is a safe place for a dog.

You'll need to find a comfortable place in the house where your Rottie can settle in and feel safe and secure. Decide where he will sleep, eat his meals, and spend most of his time. Choose a location in your yard that he will use as his bathroom area. Your pup needs his own special areas to claim as his own.

Study each room of your home and locate any items that could spell danger

In-ground waste-disposal systems make yard cleanup easy and environmentally friendly. Utilizing enzyme and bacteria action, these miniature septic tanks turn doggy waste into biodegradable ground-absorbed liquid that you never have to deal with again. The only challenge is digging a hole in the ground to accommodate the container.

it's a
Fact

if your Rottie discovers them. To avoid worrying about the puppy damaging your valuable or precious possessions or causing harm to himself, think about packing these things away and storing them for a few years, or at least until your Rottie is out of the chewing stage and fully house-trained. You also can simply declare certain rooms off limits to the dog.

Moving to a new home is a big transition for a puppy because he's leaving behind the only life he's ever known. To help your pup mature into a stable, well-adjusted adult, it's up to you to replace the warmth and security he felt with his mother and litter-mates. You'll need lots of love and plenty of patience for your pup's first few nights in his new home, but think of it as the beginning of a long and happy life together.

PUPPY-PROOFING

Get your camera ready, because you'll want to record your pup's earliest days with the family. But before you can begin the home-coming celebration, make sure that his new digs are safe. This means taking adequate measures to prevent your Rottie from find-ing trouble in his new surroundings.

Rottie-proof the inside as well as the outside of your home. Known for their intel-ligence, Rottweilers typically will want to investigate everything. Your Rottie puppy will innocently play tug with bedspreads, chomp on your best pair of shoes, and put his mouth on just about anything with an interesting taste or texture. Close doors or use baby gates to block your dog from accessing those rooms that you don't want him venturing into.

In the yard, your pup will show inter-est in digging or chewing plants, jumping on the outdoor furniture, and playing with the sprinklers. Just because you have a securely fenced-in yard doesn't guarantee that your Rottie won't figure out how to dig his way out. Take extra precautions to make sure that the gates or fencing don't have any gaps that your puppy can squeeze through.

Here are some potential hazards in your home that require your attention:

Electrical cords and wiring: All loose electrical cords must be bundled together. Building- and home-supply stores sell vari-ous types of organizing systems to hide electrical cord clutter and keep the wires out of reach. When you're not using your appliances, unplug them and insert plastic covers into all electrical outlets.

Trash cans: Keep tight-fitting lids on bathroom and kitchen garbage cans. Better yet, store them in cabinets with child-safe locks. It's near impossible to train a Rottie to leave the trash alone, especially when you're not in the room to watch him.

Household cleaners: Store all of your

NOTABLE & QUOTABLE

When our Rottie, Juneau, was seven months old, we added a few pigs to our country home. We introduced them through the fence before taking Juneau into the pasture with us, but they weren't too interested in one another. Now Juneau brings them her tennis ball to play, but the pigs still ignore her.
— Samantha Miller, Rottweiler owner in Summerville, South Carolina

The term "puppy-proofing" applies to Rotties of all ages and must be done indoors and out.

To prevent your dog from getting into the trash, use a container with a locking lid or keep it in a closed cupboard or somewhere out of his reach. Rotties can figure out how to open cabinet doors, so install childproof latches. Take any food garbage out right away, as discarded food in the trash can will draw him to the scent.

household chemicals on high shelves, out of your dog's reach.

Pest control sprays and poisons: Products that kill insects and rodents are poisonous to dogs, too. If your Rottie chews on the packaging or walks into a pest trap, he can become violently ill. Don't leave products lying around; put them in a locked cabinet. Consider using less harmful organic pest-control methods.

Houseplants: Plants add beauty to your home, but many can be dangerous to your Rottweiler. Indoor potted trees can fall on your dog, causing injury, and some plants are toxic if your dog ingests them. Fertilizers and mulch can be poisonous, too; some dogs like to dig up garden areas and hide their toys where these products are used. If you must use these products in your yard, use them only in areas that the dog cannot access.

Fabric and clothing: Dogs love sniffing, chewing, and ripping up socks, underwear, and other pieces of clothing. Don't leave clothes lying around, as fibers can cause intestinal blockage. Make sure that all members of the family pick up after themselves.

Prescriptions, painkillers, supplements, and vitamins: Don't leave any medications out on tables or countertops. Your Rottie will think that they are treats and will gobble them up, which will make him ill. Pills dropped on the floor can be deadly. Open medications over the sink, and keep all containers tightly closed and stored in medicine cabinets, out of your dog's reach. Also teach your Rottie the *leave it* cue (see chapter 10) as a precaution; this will come in handy in many situations.

Leftover food and beverages: Get in the habit of cleaning up half-full glasses of liquids, leftover food, and dirty dishes, or your Rottie will clean up for you. Some things, such as stone fruit pits and alcohol, can make your dog sick. Other foods, including chocolate, can even be fatal to dogs. There's a risk of injury, too; your dog can cut himself if he knocks over and breaks a glass or dish.

Holiday decorations: Keep Christmas tree ornaments, presents, lights, tinsel, candles, and other decorations out of your dog's reach; any of these objects can cause injury or can be lethal if swallowed. Chewing on pine needles or lapping up water out of the tree stand can cause intestinal distress.

Miscellaneous loose items: Trust your Rottweiler to chew on anything left on the floor or within his reach. This includes cell phones, remote controls, children's toys, wallets, laptops, and game pieces. Even the drywall, carpeting, and kitchen cabinets are fair game. You name it, and he can destroy it. To avoid serious injury to your dog and damage to your possessions, keep the clutter off floors and furniture.

PET-SUPPLY STORE SHOPPING LIST

In addition to making a safe home for your new addition, you'll need to do a little shopping for doggy supplies. You should be

Before you bring your Rottweiler home, make sure that you don't have anything that can put him in harm's way. Go to Club Rottie and download a list of poisonous plants and foods to avoid. Log on to **DogChannel.com/Club-Rottie** and click on "Downloads."

prepared with the basics before your new Rottie comes home.

Crate: A sturdy crate is indispensable. It aids in house-training, makes a comfy bed, and offers a safe retreat. Crates are available in hard-sided, wire, and soft collapsible styles. A hard-sided crate offers more protection for your dog during car travel and household commotion than a wire crate, and if you plan to do any air travel with your dog, you'll need an airline-approved hard-sided crate. This type of crate keeps your dog warm in cold weather but tends to heat up during summer months.

Wire crates fold up for easy transport, and they provide good air circulation. You can drape the top and sides with a sheet to give your dog a more secure, den-like feeling. The soft collapsible crate offers the most portability, but a Rottweiler that wants to escape badly enough can easily rip and chew his way out of this type of crate.

Choose a sturdy crate that's big enough for an adult Rottweiler to stand up, turn around, and lie down in comfortably. You can use dividers to adjust the crate's size while your Rottie is a puppy.

Bed: The crate will be your puppy's bed initially, but once he is past the chewing stage, he'll appreciate a separate soft pet bed. Beds are made from various materials; purchase a large one that allows your Rottie to curl up comfortably.

Leash: To take your Rottie out walking, buy a sturdy 6-foot leather or nylon leash. Avoid a retractable leash because you can't control your dog once the leash is fully extended. It also encourages dogs to pull.

Collar: Choose a sturdy adjustable buckle collar. Avoid using a choke or slip collar unless you're attaching a leash to it; otherwise, the empty ring can catch on something and your dog can choke. Snap collars often detach without warning, so avoid these types, too. The collar should fit snugly when you buy it; you should be able to fit two fingers between the dog's neck and the collar. If you have a Rottweiler puppy, be prepared to buy a larger collars as he grows.

ID tag and microchip: An identification tag should include your name and phone number. A microchip is a tiny device implanted under the dog's skin that can be scanned by police, veterinarians, or animal-shelter workers for its unique code, which is registered to you. Microchips and canine global positioning systems add extra protection to dogs should their collars or ID tags fall off.

Bowls: Purchase two bowls: one for food and one for water. Stainless steel is sturdy and long lasting and is easy to clean.

Dog gates: Dog gates, or even baby gates, help keep your Rottie out of rooms that you don't want him to have access to. Choose a model that's easy for you to open and close. Vertical bars help prevent your Rottweiler from climbing out.

Toys: Teething Rottweiler puppies have strong jaws and need to chew. To encourage your Rottie to chomp on his own toys rather than your possessions, supply him with an interesting assortment of durable toys designed for large-breed dogs. Include strong ropes, treat-dispensing toys, and nylon and hard rubber playthings that are too large for him to swallow. Select the strongest toys that you can find, with no small parts that can possibly break off and be swallowed. Avoid letting your dog chew on stuffed or squeaky toys, as a Rottweiler can quickly tear these apart and ingest the stuffing or noisemakers, which can be dangerous.

Give your pup only a few toys at a time, and rotate them regularly. Your Rottie will be excited every time you dig into his toy chest because he thinks he's getting new playthings.

Cleaning supplies: Even the best house-training efforts will be met with a few accidents. Use enzymatic cleaning products designed for pet messes, as these contain proteins that break down stains and dissolve odors. Eliminating the odor discourages your dog from returning to the same spot to relieve himself.

In the yard, get in the habit of picking up your dog's feces daily, preferably immediately after he eliminates. Dispose of waste in biodegradable bags or sealed containers. Check the yard every day for any dead rodents or debris that may have found their way into your yard and promptly dispose of it.

Extras: Once you've stocked up on the basics, expect that your Rottweiler will need other supplies along the way, such as grooming tools and flea/tick and heartworm preventives. Because every Rottie zeroes in on his favorite kinds of toys, you'll likely be replenishing your dog's collection on a regular basis when you notice any toys becoming worn.

COMING HOME

After the age of nine weeks, your Rottie pup is ready to leave the breeder and join your family. If possible, arrange to pick him up early in the morning so that you have the day to spend together and get to know one another before it's time for bed. It's even better if you can take a few days off or pick up the puppy at the start of a weekend. He'll need time to settle in and adjust to you, your family, and your household before you have to leave him and go back to work.

Before heading home with your puppy, spend some time playing with him and becoming acquainted at the breeder's home; this helps ease his transition. Bring a small blanket or an article of your clothing with you and rub it over the puppy, his littermates, and his mother. Your familiar scent will help soothe him on the ride home and throughout his first few nights in your home.

Don't bring your Rottweiler home right before a holiday. Most families are too busy celebrating to give the puppy the time and patience he needs to adjust to his new home. For this reason, reputable breeders won't let puppies leave for new homes during holiday times.

The first day home can be overwhelming for a new pup. While it's tempting to show him off to all of the neighbors and extended family as soon as he walks in the door, delay the introductions for a few days. Human interaction will be a vital part of your dog's socialization, but right now he just needs to bond with you and get used to his new home. Too much commotion will only confuse him. Just earlier that day, he was romping with his littermates, surrounded by the familiarity of his birthplace. Now his world looks radically different.

Before bringing your Rottweiler home, call a family meeting and discuss the dog-care duties. Divide the responsibilities among the family members and make sure that everyone understands what it means to raise a Rottweiler. With adult supervision, older children can help, but they should never be expected to handle all of your dog's needs.

Expect that your dog may be confused, disoriented, or even frightened by trying to figure out who you are, where he is, and what's happening to him.

If you have other pets in the home, put your new Rottie on a leash and introduce them to him one at a time. Choose a neutral location—somewhere other than the house or yard, such as a park or a neighbor's yard. If you have another dog, avoid introducing them in an area where you regularly walk your resident dog, as he may view the spot as his territory and may not welcome the intruder.

If you're adopting a Rottweiler from a rescue group or shelter, ask if you can bring your first dog to greet your new dog there. Let both dogs sniff one another for a few minutes, and keep your voice happy and friendly. Your tone of voice should send a message that you're not worried, so the dogs shouldn't be, either.

Ask your resident dog to sit or stay, and then give each dog a treat. Take them for a short walk together and let them sniff and investigate one another, all the while keeping up the happy talk and giving treats from time to time.

Once you're at home, supervise the dogs' interaction with each other. Keep both on leash until they seem comfortable with one another. Support the dominant dog in the household by letting him take over a treasured toy or special sleeping spot. If you've brought home a puppy who's being pesky, be sure to give your resident dog some time away from the newcomer.

Introduce your new Rottie to any children in the household without too much fanfare. Explain to the kids that the puppy, or even adult dog, may be frightened and that they should keep their voices low and calm, as screaming or loud noises will scare the dog even more. Don't expect him to play right away because he needs time to settle in.

With the Rottie on a leash held by you or another responsible adult, children should sit on the floor and let the dog approach them. Control the dog so that he doesn't jump up. If the children are old enough, let them offer a few treats or a new toy. They should be taught to pet him gently and should not reach out and grab the dog.

Allow everyone a chance to spend some private time with the pup. Let him sniff and explore his surroundings. Walk him through all of the rooms in the house and spend some time with him in the yard.

Don't be concerned if your Rottie doesn't want to eat or drink much the first day. By the second day, he should have his appetite back. As he's adjusting to his new home, speak reassuring words to him and be patient.

FIRST NIGHT HOME

A pup's first day in his new home can be exhausting. More than likely, he'll take a nap or two during the day, but hold off putting him to bed for the night until an hour or two before you're ready to turn in.

The kids will be excited to welcome the new puppy home; be sure to supervise their time together to ensure that all goes well.

Some ordinary household items make great toys for your Rottweiler—as long you make sure that they are safe. Tennis balls, plastic water bottles, old towels, and more can be transformed into fun with a little creativity. You can find a list of homemade toys at **DogChannel.com/Club-Rottie.**

Play with your Rottie to tire him out, and take him outside to potty one last time right before bedtime.

Many puppies whine and cry at night, especially if they're isolated from their new people in another room. Avoid this problem by putting your Rottweiler's crate next to your bed. Your presence helps reassure your pup during the night that he's not alone.

Your new Rottie pup has spent his life up to this point jockeying for position alongside his littermates and mother. Now that he doesn't have these snuggle partners to lean up against, he feels especially lonely. To make the transition easier on him, give him a plush toy about the size of one of his littermates to bunk with. While your puppy knows that the stuffed animal isn't a real brother or sister, it's something soft and warm that he can cuddle up with at night. For extra reassurance, add a piece of bedding from his former home or an article of clothing that has the scent of his littermates on it. Put one or two chew toys in the crate so if he wakes up during the night, he can amuse himself without disturbing you.

If your puppy whimpers during the night, whisper soft comforting words to him, but do not take him out of his crate and let him sleep on the bed with you, no matter how much he fusses and no matter how hard it is for you to resist. Sleeping on your bed becomes a bad habit that's difficult to break, and it doesn't teach your Rottie self-reliance.

He shouldn't need to relieve himself for three or four hours after going to bed. Young puppies don't have the capacity to "hold it" for a full eight hours, so if you think he has to go outside to eliminate, quietly take him out. Resist the urge to talk to him or he'll think it's playtime; make this a "strictly business" trip outside.

When you come back in, put him right back inside the crate. Within a few nights, your puppy will adjust to his new sleeping routine and should remain quiet for a six- or seven-hour stretch. Training your dog to sleep in his crate or, once he's housetrained, on a blanket or in a dog bed on the floor helps establish you as the authority.

NOTABLE & QUOTABLE

For a puppy's first night, I like to put a wire crate in our bedroom next to our bed and let him sleep in it. This way, I can hear him if he needs to go potty during the night. When I put my hand up against the crate, he senses that I'm nearby and doesn't feel so lonely.

—Kathy Yontz, a Rottweiler breeder in Springfield, Ohio

Good behavior begins at home, and an essential part of household etiquette is appropriate potty manners. Your Rottweiler wants to please you, especially when it comes to relieving himself in the right place at the right time. The breed is no more difficult to house-train than others, but it's your job is to make the process as easy as possible for your dog. If your instructions are clear, your Rottie will comply.

When it comes to teaching your puppy where to go to the bathroom, there's no magic involved; there are just a few basic principles that you'll need to follow. The keys to successful house-training are prevention, vigilance, praise, and patience. You'll also need a crate, a leash, and clean-up supplies.

THE BASIC PROCESS

When you bring your Rottweiler home, he won't have a clue where you want him to relieve himself. When he lived with his littermates and mother, he had a favorite

Middle-aged and older Rotties who are obese have more trouble controlling their bladder activity. Even if completely house-trained, overweight dogs will frequently leak and dribble urine without meaning to. This condition, known as incontinence, may be the result of other medical problems.

it's a
Fact

potty location. Now, in his new home, everything has an unfamiliar smell, and there are new textures beneath his feet. It should come as no surprise, then, that he'll go to the bathroom wherever he feels comfortable.

Begin training your Rottweiler, whether puppy or adult, to relieve himself outdoors the moment you bring him home. Rottweilers are intelligent, and they're capable of being house-trained at an early age, although you can house-train a dog at any time.

Choose a Spot

To make the process an easy one, choose a designated bathroom spot outside that's easily accessible. Take your Rottie out on a leash to the designated area as soon as you bring him home, and remain standing there with him. When he's finished checking out the odors around him, he'll do his business. If you walk around with your dog rather than staying in the specific potty area, he'll continue to be stimulated by new smells, which only prolongs his search for the right spot.

Select a verbal cue that you will use every time you take your Rottweiler outside to potty. Tell him something such as "Hurry up" or "Get it done," and he'll begin to associate urinating or defecating with hearing those words. Be sure to pick a phrase that you feel comfortable saying in public.

When he goes, praise him lavishly. Tell him "Good dog" in an upbeat, happy tone of voice whenever he goes outside.

Use a Crate

To prevent house-training accidents, introduce your Rottweiler to a crate or an exercise pen ("X-pen"). Such an enclosure provides a safe, comfy spot in which to contain your dog when you can't keep an eye on him or when he just needs some down time. The crate or pen should be just large enough to allow your Rottie to turn around and lie down without having to curl up; if using a crate, your dog should also be able to stand up fully without hitting his head on the top.

Don't use a crate or a pen with too much empty space. Dogs won't potty where they sleep because they don't like to lie in their own urine or feces. If you have a puppy in a too-large crate, he will eliminate at one end of the crate and lie down at the other end. Using an appropriately sized crate helps your Rottweiler develop bladder and bowel control.

When you let your dog out of the crate, he'll need to eliminate, so take him to the designated outdoor location right away. After a few trips, he'll figure out the routine and will learn to hold it until you release him from the crate.

Introducing the crate to your Rottie should be a positive experience. You want him to like his new den, so it's important to start off correctly. It is hoped that your breeder gave the puppies a crate to sleep in or your adopted adult came from a home in which he was crate-trained, as this will help your Rottie adjust to his new crate more quickly. If not, and you have a puppy who seems fearful or an adult who had been isolated for long hours in his crate in his previous home, crate-training your Rottie in your home will take a while. Instead, start off with an exercise pen or baby playpen until he's more willing to accept new ideas.

Place the crate in the room where you and your family spend the most time. Rottweilers are social creatures and want

Once your Rottie is crate-trained, you'll find the crate useful for many purposes, such as traveling.

Sometimes when older unneutered males come into rescue, they'll mark in the house. It takes a while to retrain them, but eventually they figure it out. They're working dogs who want to please you.

—Victoria Wiltsie, Rottweiler owner and member of Gulfstream Guardian Angels Rottweiler Rescue in Miami, Florida

to feel like part of the family. Seeing you move around or just hanging out gives your dog a secure feeling. At night, move the crate next to your bed, or purchase a second crate to keep in your bedroom.

Begin crate-training on the day you bring your new Rottie home. Place a soft blanket, one of your old shirts with your scent, a few toys, and a blanket or toy from his former home inside the crate. Be aware, though, that a Rottie pup will chew, so don't put anything inside that your pup can easily shred and choke on.

If you have a wire crate for your Rottweiler, place a sheet over the top and sides to give it a cozier feel and to help the pup learn to be comfortable in a small area. Take your Rottie's collar off when he's in the wire crate, as his identification tags can get caught.

Teaching your puppy to love his crate is easy. All you need is time, patience, and the confidence that you are doing the right thing for him. To crate your dog:

1. Open the door and let him approach and sniff as much or as little as he wants. Show him a crunchy treat and place it inside the crate, at the front. If he takes it, praise him.

2. Repeat the first step a few times, and then toss a treat inside so that it hits the back of the crate and makes a noise. Tell your Rottie "Go get it!" When he walks all the way into the crate to get the treat, make a huge fuss over him.

3. Toss another treat to the back of the crate, and when he goes in after it, close the crate door for a few seconds. Talk to your Rottie and tell him what a good dog he is. Open the door and give him another treat when he comes out of the crate. Repeat a few more times, increasing the time that you keep the door closed.

4. Give your Rottweiler his meal inside the crate. Close the crate door and stay with him while he's eating. When he's finished, let him out and praise him. At the next mealtime, feed him inside the crate but leave the room while he's eating. Return when he's finished to let him out and praise him. Repeat with a few more meals, leaving him in the crate after he's finished a little longer each time.

5. Put your Rottie in the crate without a meal—throw a treat to the back of the crate and tell him to "Go get it!"—and close the door. Be sure to For the first few times, stay in the room but don't

How often does a Rottweiler puppy do his business? A lot! Go to **DogChannel.com/Club-Rottie** and download the typical potty schedule of a puppy. You can also download a chart that you can fill out to track your dog's elimination timetable, which will help you with house-training.

JOIN OUR ONLINE
Club Rottie™

When you take your Rottie outside for a potty trip, walk him directly to the designated area.

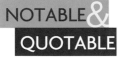
Before taking Riley on a road trip with us to visit friends in another state, we bought him a soft-sided crate. Big mistake. One night, we went out and left him in the crate in their home. When we came back, he was running loose in the house. He had chewed through the crate, completely destroying it.

—Christy Brown, pet massage therapist in Colorado Springs. Colorado

talk to him. The next few times, walk out of the room and return a few minutes later. Gradually extend the time that he's inside with you out of the room. Always praise your dog for remaining quiet in his crate.

While a crate has many advantages, it should never be overused. Once crate-trained, your Rottie should never be crated for longer than five or six hours at a time during the day. At night, while he's asleep, a longer duration isn't a problem.

Make a Schedule

To house-train your Rottweiler, set up a schedule and stick to it. Your Rottie will not need as many potty trips throughout the day as he grows and is able to hold it for longer periods of time.

1. Let your dog out of the crate or pen first thing in the morning and bring him outside for a potty trip.
2. Feed him his morning meal and take him outside right after he eats.
3. Bring him back inside the house and watch him closely. If he drinks water, take him outside again. If he displays body language, such as sniffing the ground or walking in circles, signaling that he needs to go to the bathroom, quickly whisk him out the door.
4. Take your puppy outside about once every hour when he's awake and active. Older dogs can hold it longer.
5. If he's ready for a nap, take him outside before putting him into the crate.
6. After he wakes up, take him outside again.
7. Repeat Steps 3 and 4 throughout the day.
8. Take him outside after his evening meal and again before he goes to bed.

SOLUTIONS FOR COMMON PROBLEMS

If you think that your Rottweiler is taking a long time to get the hang of house-training, go back to basics. Be vigilant about putting your dog inside his crate when you can't watch him, and be sure to promptly take him outside to eliminate every time you let him out of his crate.

Don't confine him in the crate for too long. During the day, most three-month-old puppies can hold their bladders in the crate for about three hours, but some will need to go out more frequently.

Pay close attention to your puppy while he's out of the crate and playing in the house. If you give him too much freedom before he's fully house-trained, he'll have accidents.

Unless you catch your dog in the act of relieving himself in the house, it's best to completely ignore the accident and quietly clean it up. If you do catch him in the act, tell him "No" and get him outside immediately so that he can finish his business

Did You Know? Dogs who start to urinate more frequently or who suddenly begin having accidents, either during the day or while sleeping, may have a kidney, liver, or reproductive problem. Your veterinarian can rule out or confirm any issues by performing laboratory tests that include a urinalysis, a complete blood count, and X-ray imaging.

Having house-training problems with your Rottie? Ask other Rottie owners for advice and tips, or post your own success story to give other owners encouragement. Log on to **DogChannel.com/Club-Rottie** and click on "Community."

in the proper place. Rubbing your dog's nose in the mess, yelling, or hitting your dog doesn't work. He'll resort to sneaking behind the furniture or going into a corner to avoid being seen when he eliminates.

When you take your dog out, always stay with him and watch him to make sure that he relieves himself. If left alone in the yard, your Rottie may become distracted and forget why he's there, and you won't be sure if he's actually gone to the bathroom.

Be aware that medical problems may cause increased urination, urinary incontinence, or difficulty in urinating. Cushing's disease, bladder stones, a urinary tract infection, chronic kidney failure, brain or spinal cord injury, diabetes, and some medications, such as prednisone, can affect urination. If your Rottie seems to regress in his house-training or is not responding to your training efforts, visit your vet.

DOMINANT AND SUBMISSIVE URINATION

Unneutered males sometimes develop the annoying habit of marking territory. Some dominant females might behave like this as well. The behavior may crop up for several reasons—for example, if there's a change in the family structure, if the dominant dog leaves, or if a new dog joins the household. While neutering a male helps, it may not eliminate the behavior completely.

If your Rottweiler marks in the home, constantly supervise him and confine the dog if you cannot watch him. If you observe your dog marking in the house, don't punish him, but quickly get his attention by calling his name and distracting him.

When your Rottweiler meets you, a family member, or a visitor to your home by crouching, averting eye contact, and dribbling some urine, it's a behavior issue, not a house-training problem. This behavior is called submissive or excited urination; dogs of any age, but mostly puppies and young female dogs, will urinate during greetings. Submissive urination is a combination of instinctive and learned behaviors.

Timid, insecure Rotties will urinate to express appeasement and deference when greeting a superior pack member as a way of deflecting possible aggression. Some dogs may be just too excited to hold their urine. Dogs in rescue situations may behave this way, and it becomes a habit when they go to new homes.

When owners react to submissive urination by reprimanding the dog, it only intensifies the submissive response. The best solution is to modify the way you greet your dog to encourage a calmer method. Avoid leaning over your dog as you greet him. Pet his chest instead of his head. Better yet, let your dog approach you instead of you approaching him. When you first enter the house, either ignore him completely or speak softly in a low, calm tone. After fifteen minutes or so, minutes he'll calm down, accept your arrival, and forget his need to show his submissive side.

CLEAN-UP TIPS

Dogs will return to areas where they or other dogs have urinated or defecated to

Always clean up after your Rottweiler, whether in your own yard or a public place.

A common house-training mistake is allowing a young puppy run of the house. This is a vast environment from the puppy's point of view, an open invitation to have accidents. Puppies have no inhibition about eliminating where they play.

—Susan Meluzin, a professional dog handler and trainer in Flushing, New York

leave their own mark. If your dog has an accident in the house, removing the mess as well as the odor prevents him from wanting to go there again. Although you can use a black light to show old urine stains, you can probably use your nose and eyes to find soiled areas.

The sooner you clean up an accident, the easier and more thoroughly you can remove the odor. Pick up any solids with a plastic bag, and use paper towels to absorb liquid before applying a cleaning product.

An enzymatic cleaner made for pet messes is the most effective. Available in pet-supply stores and nontoxic to pets, this product contains proteins that break down stains and dissolve odors. After using the product, place plastic wrap over the area to prevent it from drying out, and place a chair over the area to prohibit your dog's access. After about an hour, remove the chair and discard the plastic.

Avoid using a steam cleaner to dissipate urine odors from carpet or upholstery. The heat permanently sets the odor by bonding the proteins to the fibers. Ammonia or vinegar doesn't work, either. To a dog, these products smell like urine and encourage him to mark again. If you have soiled small rugs that are machine washable, add a box of baking soda to your regular detergent.

For urine burns on your grass, remove the damaged grass, reseed, and cover with compost. Water the area regularly and give the grass some time to grow. It isn't the pH of your dog's urine that kills the grass; it's the nitrogen in the urine, which is a natural byproduct of protein metabolism.

To decrease urine burn naturally, make sure that your Rottie is well hydrated. Give your dog more opportunities to urinate, as smaller amounts will decrease the potential for damage. Flush the lawn with fresh water right after your dog urinates.

Female Marking

When Bubbles first came to the Second Chance Rottweiler Rescue in Davis, California, the female Rottie urinated on everything in her foster family's house. Immediately, Elaine Greenberg, president of the organization, began house-training her.

"I began with the basics, including crate-training," Greenberg says. "She never urinated in her crate, but as soon as I let her out, she would sniff and urinate before I could get her outside. Bubbles even lifts her leg just like a male. She hikes it higher than the boys and practically does a handstand on her front feet."

Rescue volunteers suspect that the four-year-old Rottie once lived with intact males who marked in the house and that she probably learned her bad bathroom habits from them.

Greenberg tried putting panties on Bubbles while she was in the house, thinking that they would help deter her. "She didn't care about piddling in her pants, so after a few weeks, I [stopped using them]. I've worked with rescue Rotties since 1964, and she's the only one I've ever had a hard time house-training. Otherwise, she's such a great dog, and I'd never think of giving up on her. She's sweet and friendly, great with puppies and other dogs, walks beautifully on the leash without puling, and is so pretty to look at."

Eventually Greenberg's persistence started to pay off. "After working on this for at least six months, I think she's turning a house-training corner. Now, when I take her out of the crate and put her leash on right away, she doesn't even try to sniff until we're outside," she says.

Did You Know?

Pet waste left on grass or roadways makes its way to storm drains when it rains. Storm drains lead to lakes or streams that flow into reservoirs and the drinking-water supply. Dog feces may carry disease-causing organisms, making water unsanitary for swimming and expensive to treat for drinking.

CHAPTER 6

GET TO KNOW

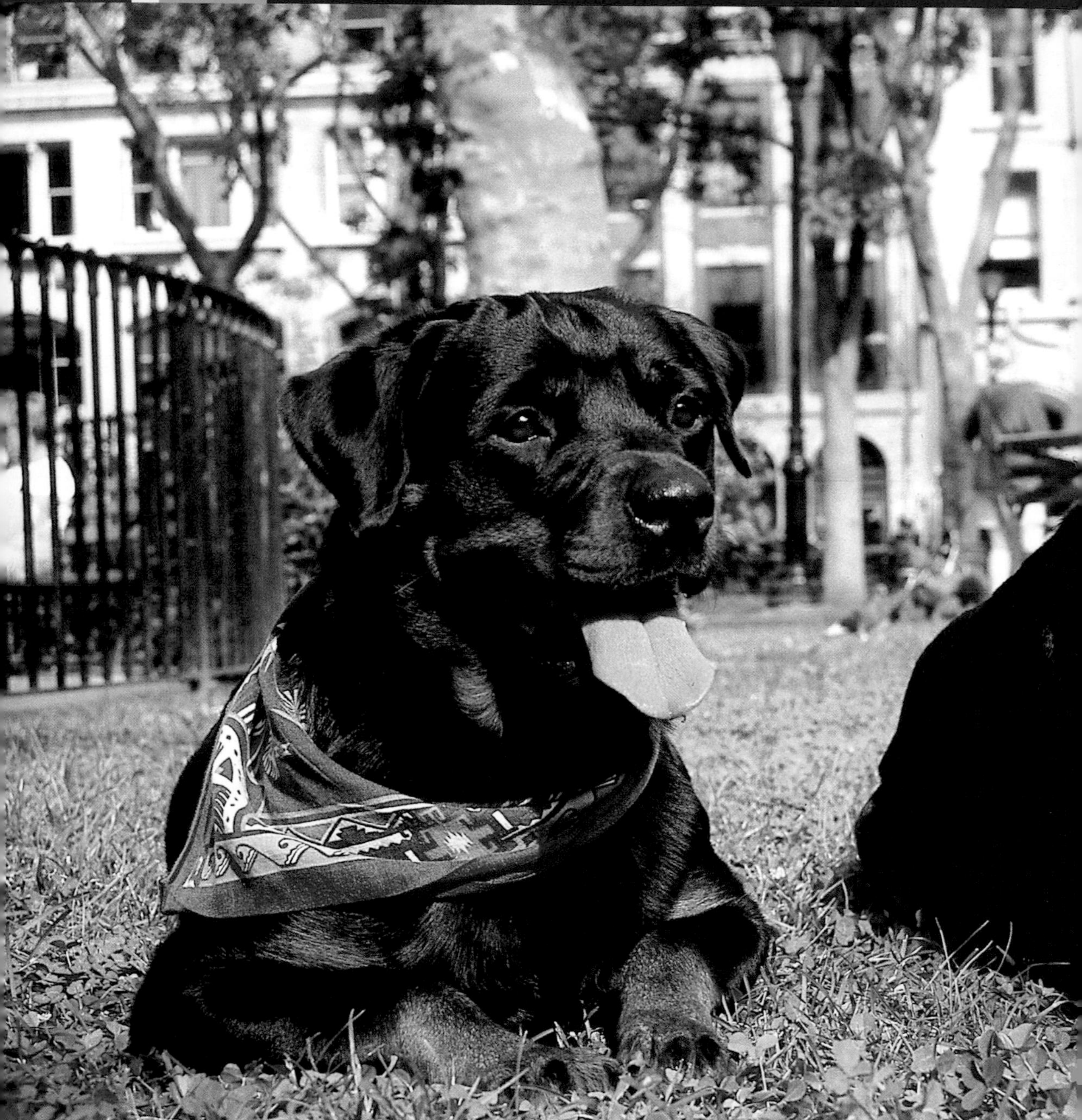

YOUR VET

Sometimes it takes a village to keep your Rottweiler in tip-top shape. Keeping your dog healthy and active throughout his life begins with a knowledgeable veterinarian and a conscientious office staff. As your dog ages, you'll rely on these professionals to provide the right vaccines at the right times, advise you on preventive-health measures, and help you deal with any health problems that your Rottie may experience.

SELECTING A VET

Choosing a good veterinarian who understands Rottweilers and feels comfortable treating them is one of the most important decisions that you will make for your dog. Your chosen vet must also be an expert in detecting illnesses and up-to-date on the latest veterinary research. When visiting the veterinarian with your dog, you should

A dog's normal temperature is between 100.5 and 102.5 degrees Fahrenheit (38 and 39.2 degrees Celsius). A body temperature over 104 or under 99 degrees Fahrenheit indicates an emergency situation. Moderate heat stroke occurs when a dog's temperature is between 103 and 106 degrees Fahrenheit. Use a canine ear thermometer to measure your Rottweiler's temperature.

it's a
Fact

never feel rushed, and the office should always appear clean and orderly. Choose a vet who clearly explains medical terms and answers all of your questions, thus making it easy to develop a rapport.

If you haven't already chosen a veterinarian by the time your new Rottie comes home, you'll need to do so immediately. Within the first 48 hours of bringing your Rottie home, he needs to visit the doctor for his first checkup.

Start your veterinarian search by asking your breeder for a referral. Even if your breeder doesn't live nearby, reputable breeders maintain a network of other breeders across the country that should be able to recommend good veterinarians. Members of a local Rottweiler club or kennel club can also share the names of veterinarians they trust. Referrals from other Rottweiler owners are helpful, too. If there's a college of veterinary medicine near you, contact it for a list of nearby veterinarians who may be affiliated with the school. Check out accredited animal hospitals online at the American Animal Hospital Association (AAHA) website (www.healthypet.com).

The ideal veterinary practice should be conveniently located and offer office hours that work with your schedule. It is hoped that your Rottweiler will never have an emergency, but if he does, your vet's office should have after-hours care or should recommend a nearby emergency facility.

Schedule a time to visit the veterinary offices that you're considering. A good clinic will give you a free tour of the facilities, which gives you a good behind-the-scenes look at the efficiency and cleanliness of the practice. Look at the veterinarians' diplomas hanging on the walls. These should be from accredited veterinary colleges, and the doctors should be members of professional veterinary associations, such as the American Veterinary Medical Association (AVMA) or a state or local veterinary association. Ask if the office has a computerized billing and file system, as this facilitates easy access to your dog's medical history. However, the most important factor in choosing a veterinarian and clinic is whether you feel comfortable taking your dog there for a visit.

If you're ever unsure about your veterinarian's diagnosis or level of care, take your dog to another veterinarian for a second opinion. Some conditions are beyond a general-practice veterinarian's area of expertise. In these cases, the vet should refer you to a veterinary specialist or nearby veterinary school.

Today, veterinary specialty clinics operate in many disciplines, including dermatology, cardiology, dentistry, ophthalmology, orthopedics, oncology, and neurosurgery. These specialists have high-tech medical equipment and can perform advanced diagnostic testing that is an important tool for treating difficult cases and can often

Your—and your Rottie's—rapport with a veterinarian is one of the most important factors when deciding on a vet.

Spaying and neutering decreases the risk of some canine cancers, but recent research shows that the procedures actually increase the risk of other types. Another study claims that spaying and neutering before six months of age is responsible for the development of cruciate ligament tears, urinary incontinence, hip dysplasia, and hypothyroidism. Talk to your veterinarian about the pros and cons.

— Debra Eldredge, DVM, a veterinarian in Vernon, New York

save a dog's life. While seeing a specialist may be more expensive than a visit to your general-practice veterinarian, your dog will receive the benefits of the veterinarian's specialized training in the given field and the latest medical advances. To locate a veterinary specialist, refer to the AVMA website (www.avma.org) and click on "veterinary specialty organizations."

YOUR FIRST VET VISIT

Schedule an appointment for your dog so that he sees the vet within a day or two of coming home. Bring along your Rottie's vaccination and worming record, a fresh stool sample, and his blanket from home, as a comfort item helps reduce your dog's stress level. Show your Rottie what a fun place the vet's office is by arriving a few minutes early to give him plenty of time to look around, sniff the surroundings, and greet the staff. You may have to fill out some paperwork while you're waiting, and you don't want to feel rushed.

During this first visit, the veterinarian will establish a bond with your dog by performing an examination. During the exam, the doctor will take your dog's temperature, weigh him, and evaluate his overall appearance. The doctor will feel his abdomen and other body parts to check for normal development; examine your Rottie's skin for any abnormal bumps, sores, or pests; and look into his eyes and ears. Checking your dog's mouth will indicate whether the gums and teeth are healthy, and listening to your dog's heart and lungs will reveal any potential circulatory problems. If you have a male, the veterinarian will make sure that the testicles have descended or are retained in the abdomen.

You should feel comfortable discussing any concerns you have about your Rottie. After the initial examination, your vet will set up a schedule for vaccinations and wormings.

VACCINATIONS

As a puppy, your Rottweiler received passive immunity, or temporary protection from certain diseases, through his mother's milk. This natural protection can last from eight to fourteen weeks. Puppies younger than eight weeks old should not be vaccinated; the mother's immunity neutralizes the vaccine, so it offers little protection against disease.

This early preventive care is the best defense against disease. Vaccination protects your dog from certain deadly communicable diseases by boosting his immune system. Derived from viruses or bacteria that have been either killed or weakened (modified live), vaccines trigger the production of antibodies, which fight future infections and provide resistance that can last for months or even years.

Core vaccines are recommended for all dogs at some point in their lives. These include vaccinations against distemper,

Did You Know? According to a study at Indiana University South Bend, 93 percent of dog owners took their pets to the veterinarian at least once a year. In interviews, many pet owners reported that their pets' health was a major concern, especially as their dogs got older. Some admitted that they spent significant amounts of money on their pets' health.

Do what you can to keep your Rottweiler cool in summer weather, as the breed can be prone to heat stroke.

Just like infants, puppies need a series of vaccinations to ensure that they stay healthy during their first year of life. Download a vaccination chart from **DogChannel.com/Club-Rottie** that you can fill out for your Rottweiler.

Basic knowledge of canine first aid helps you deal with minor injuries and illnesses at home.

canine adenovirus type-2 (hepatitis and respiratory disease), and canine parvovirus type-2. They prevent diseases that are dangerous, have a wide distribution, or are contagious to people. These should be administered at least three to four weeks apart, starting between eight and ten weeks of age.

Required by law, the rabies vaccine is also a core vaccine. It should be given at three to six months, then one year later, and then either annually or every three years, according to local law.

Noncore, or elective, vaccines include those that protect dogs against less severe infections that are treatable. These should be given to dogs who are particularly susceptible to contracting leptospirosis, coronavirus, canine parainfluenza, kennel cough (*Bordetella*), and Lyme disease. Discuss with your vet which, if any, of the noncore vaccines your dog should receive.

Veterinarians once routinely recommended revaccinating dogs every year, but new research shows that there are risks associated with annual immunizations, especially if a dog already has sufficient immunity. In 2006, the AAHA issued a new set of guidelines. For the core vaccines, a booster is recommended one year after the initial series, followed by a booster shot every three years. Booster schedules for the noncore vaccines may vary. Before vaccinating your dog, discuss the recommended protocols in your area with your vet. Request that your veterinarian perform a titer test before making the decision to booster your Rottweiler's vaccinations.

After your dog has received his initial core vaccines, the veterinarian can use a blood sample to measure the levels of protective antibodies already present in the body. This is called serum vaccine antibody titer testing.

A high titer count reveals a high level of immunity to the disease, while a low titer count shows that a dog may still be susceptible. Many veterinarians recommend using a titer test to see if a dog needs a vaccine before administering one; such tests are not available for *Bordetella*, parainfluenza, or coronavirus.

NEUTERING AND SPAYING
Neutering and spaying are terms that refer to sterilization, or the surgical removal of a dog's reproductive organs. Neutering

is done in males, while spaying is done in females. Not only do these procedures prevent unwanted puppies but they also reduce or eliminate the risk of certain health and behavioral problems.

Dogs can be spayed or neutered at any age. According to the AVMA, the procedure can be safely performed on puppies as early as eight weeks of age.

FIRST-AID KITS

It's a fact—accidents happen. To care for minor ailments and injuries and to help your dog in an emergency before you can get him to the veterinarian, be prepared to provide first-aid treatment at home. A basic first-aid kit should contain the following items:

- Antibiotic ointment
- Antiseptic and antibacterial wipes
- Antihistamine tablets
- Antacid tablets
- Blunt-tipped and sharp scissors
- Canine first-aid handbook
- Canine thermometer
- Cotton-tipped applicators
- Disposable razor
- Extra leash and collar or harness
- Eye dropper
- First-aid tape
- Gauze pads
- Hydrogen peroxide 3% USP
- Instant cold compress
- Kaopectate tablets or liquid
- Latex gloves
- Lubricating jelly
- Muzzle
- Nail clippers
- Pen and paper for notes or directions
- Phone numbers and addresses of your veterinarian and emergency clinic
- Self-adhesive bandage wrap
- Sterile saline eyewash
- Styptic powder (to stop bleeding if you cut the quick during nail trimming)
- Tweezers

EVERYDAY PROBLEMS

Observing your Rottie every day and noting any differences in his appearance and behavior will help nip problems in the bud before they become crises. It helps to keep a small notebook handy and record your dog's overall well-being every day. This makes it easier to remember the details of any illnesses he's had as he ages.

Cuts and Scrapes

Clean small cuts or scrapes with saline solution or warm water. Check for debris and carefully remove it with tweezers. Apply a small amount of antibiotic ointment to the clean wound. If a wound continues to bleed, take your Rottie to see your veterinarian.

NOTABLE & QUOTABLE

Large, active dogs who enjoy outdoor exercise can cut a paw or experience heat stroke, bee stings, snake bites, or poisoning. To treat your Rottweiler while away from home, always bring along a good first-aid kit. Learning how to administer rescue breathing and CPR techniques may help save your dog's life.
— Denise Fleck, pet first-aid expert and instructor from Los Angeles, California

Diarrhea

One or two runny stools may not be a problem. If your Rottie has diarrhea, feed him small amounts of cottage cheese, plain boiled rice, plain yogurt, and boiled chicken or turkey instead of his regular food. An over-the-counter antidiarrheal medication (such as Kaopectate) may help; contact your vet for dosing. If the diarrhea continues for more than forty-eight hours, your dog needs to see the veterinarian.

Colds

Dogs don't suffer from common colds as humans do, but they can have similar symptoms, such as coughing, sneezing, or runny noses, which can be caused by allergies or respiratory infections. If your dog has chronic symptoms, has difficulty breathing, or is producing of phlegm, take him to the vet.

Constipation

Dogs normally have one or two bowel movements per day. If you notice that your Rottweiler is straining to defecate, or if he is producing smaller than normal, hard feces, he may be constipated. While this condition may not be life threatening, it's often painful and uncomfortable. Dogs who are suffering from constipation typically don't have enough fiber in their diets, but a dog also can become constipated when stressed, such as during travel. To ease the condition, make sure that your Rottie has plenty of fresh water, receives regular exercise, and has enough opportunities to relieve himself.

Vomiting

Every once in a while, a healthy dog will vomit or have gastric upset and refuse to eat. If you notice this in your Rottie, withhold food for one or two meals. Follow that with small amounts of bland foods such as cottage cheese, plain yogurt, plain rice, or boiled chicken, ground turkey, or beef. If vomiting continues for more than two days, consult your veterinarian.

Supplement your Rottweiler's meals with grated or small pieces of fruits and vegetables that are safe for dogs to eat. You can also mix one or two tablespoons of canned pumpkin into your dog's food. If symptoms last for more than two or three days, visit the veterinarian.

No one expects a natural disaster, but planning ahead in the event that one occurs may save your Rottweiler's life. Follow these easy steps before you have to evacuate your home:

1. Post a rescue sticker (available from www.aspca.org) on your front window to let emergency personnel know that pets are inside your home. If you're away from home when disaster strikes, people will know to help your dog.
2. Choose the safest way to evacuate from your home. Identify those rooms and locations in your home that are away from flying glass or debris.
3. Keep a leash near the front and back doors so you can take your dog out of the house securely.
4. Assemble an emergency evacuation kit. Gather emergency supplies for your dog in a waterproof, easily portable container with a tight-fitting lid. Pack three to seven days' worth of nonperishable dog food, a seven-day supply of bottled water, a dog bowl, a two-week supply of any medications that your dog needs, a canine first-aid kit, and clean-up bags. Include a small pet blanket, a toy, grooming items, and a towel. A spray container of diluted household bleach comes in handy, too.
5. Make sure that your dog's collar fits snugly and that his ID tag is up-to-date and easy to read. Microchip your dog as a permanent form of identification.
6. Put a current photo and description of your dog in your evacuation kit in case you become separated from him and need to prove that he belongs to you. Also make a current list of your dog's vaccinations, any medical conditions, and behavior problems, which will provide information about your dog if he needs to be placed in foster care.
7. In case disaster strikes when you're not home, make advance arrangements with neighbors to take care of your dog until you can be reunited with him. Give them a key to your home or let them know where they can find one on your property.

If you are given an official order to evacuate your home, obey it and take your dog with you. Don't wait until the last minute!

PREPARE FOR DISASTER

CHAPTER 7

ROTTWEILER

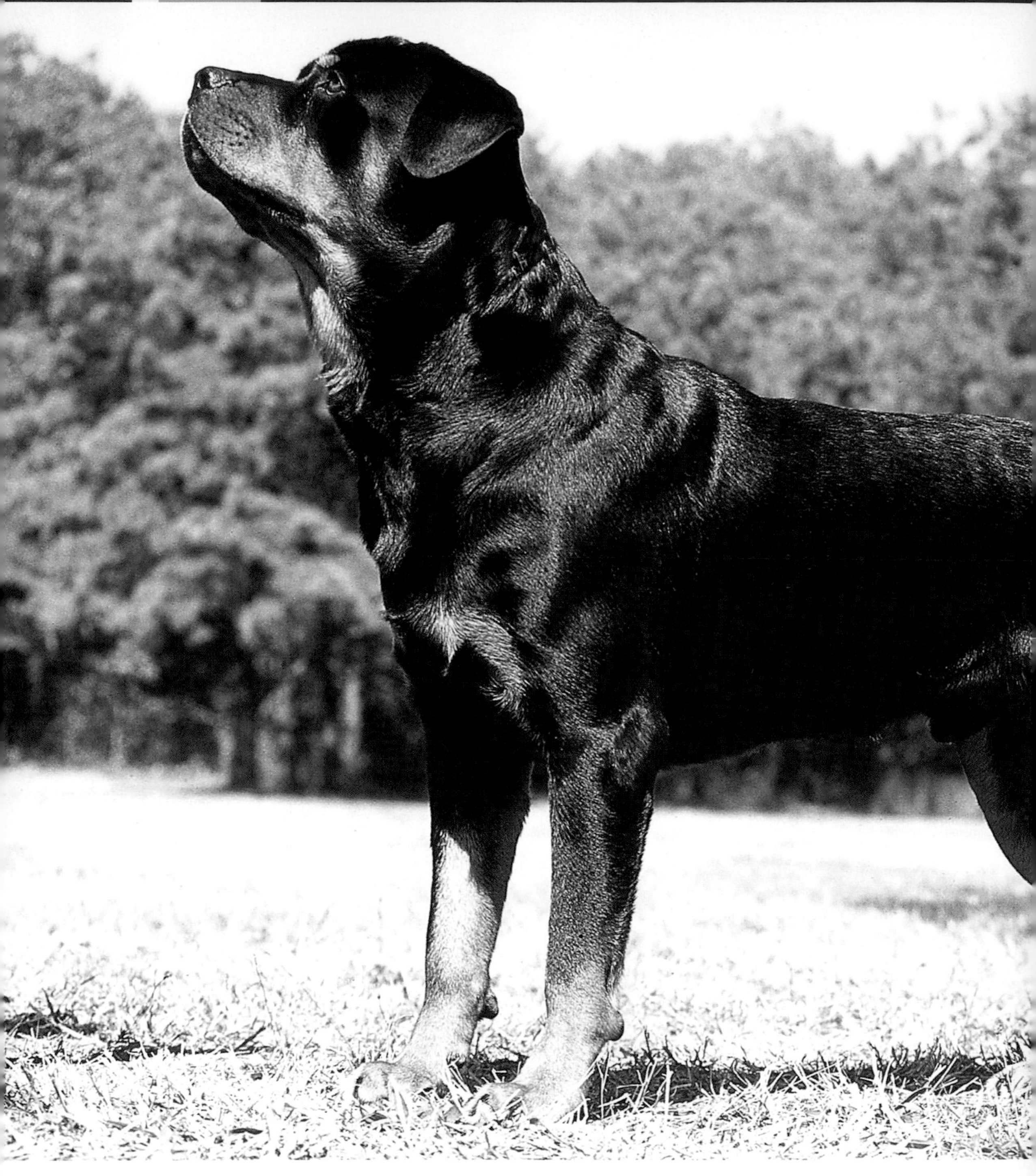

HEALTH

In a perfect world, every Rottweiler would inherit only healthy genes and live to a ripe old age, but every breed has the potential risk for at least a few genetic illnesses. When breeders pair only healthy dogs together and test their breeding stock for hereditary diseases before breeding litters, the chances of their puppies developing problems later in life are reduced. While the parents' genes play a large role in your Rottweiler's genetic health, regular veterinary checkups and early detection of problems may help prolong your dog's life.

ROTTWEILER HEALTH ISSUES

Generally, the Rottweiler is a sturdy, healthy breed, but this doesn't prevent breeders and owners from worrying about genetic problems. To improve the overall health status of the breed, the American Rottweiler Club established the Rottweiler Health Foundation in 1998. According to its mission statement, the foundation's

Did You Know?

The testicles of male puppies usually descend from the abdomen into the scrotal sac within ten days after birth. If only one descends, the dog cannot be shown in conformation, but he can reproduce. Sometimes the organs will descend by six months. Dogs with undescended testicles have a greater incidence of testicular tumors.

If your dog fails to lose weight despite eating less and exercising more, take him to the veterinarian for an examination. Hypothyroidism, Cushing's disease, and diabetes may cause increased appetite or thirst, plus other physical symptoms and behavior problems.

goal is "To raise money to fund critical research into the genetic, communicable, and acquired diseases that plague our beloved breed, the Rottweiler." Following are some of the more common hereditary problems of concern to Rottweiler breeders and fanciers.

Anterior Cruciate Ligament Ruptures

Injuries to the anterior cruciate ligament (ACL), found in the joint of the femur and the tibia, are among the most common orthopedic problems that plague dogs. A Rottie doesn't have to excel as a canine athlete to injure his knee; he can suffer a ruptured ACL through gradual weakening or degeneration.

Being overweight adds stress to the knee, causing ACL tears. Making sudden turns while running, falling on a slippery floor, and twisting the back leg can rupture the cruciate ligament. A dog who has ruptured his ACL will show stiffness and will limp. The knee may swell and the dog will hold up the affected leg.

A veterinarian diagnoses a ruptured ACL through examination, manipulation of the joint to observe the way it moves, and X-rays. Surgery can correct the problem, but the dog may develop arthritis if treatment is delayed.

Atopic Dermatitis

Canine atopic dermatitis, also known as allergic dermatitis or canine atopy, is an inherited tendency to develop allergic symptoms after exposure to an otherwise harmless substance, such as dust mites, mold, or pollen. Environmental allergens can also include weeds, grass, and leaves. Allergens in food and from parasites, such as fleas, and bacterial or yeast infections of the skin add to the problem and complicate recovery.

Many breeds suffer from atopic dermatitis; in the Rottweiler, dogs between one and three years of age are particularly sensitive. Exposure to allergens triggers an immune reaction, causing itchy and inflamed skin. Affected dogs react by rubbing, licking, chewing, biting, or scratching at their feet, muzzles, ears, armpits, or groins, which causes hair loss and red, thickened skin.

Dogs usually have problems when the pollen count is high during the spring, summer, and fall seasons. To diagnose specific atopic dermatitis, the veterinarian will observe the condition and perform a skin scraping (to rule out parasites) or blood testing. Treatment includes antihistamines, corticosteroids, or other medications; fatty acid supplements; baths with hypoallergenic shampoos; removal or avoidance of allergens; and perhaps a change in diet.

Cancer

Dogs are living longer than they ever did before, but many older dogs succumb to cancer. According to the Animal Cancer Center at Colorado State University, 50 percent of all dogs develop cancer if they live ten years or longer.

Cancer is a class of diseases in which the cells grow uncontrollably, invade the

 NOTABLE & QUOTABLE

Traditional Chinese Medicine (TCM), which includes herbs and acupuncture, as well as Western medicine can provide relief for many musculoskeletal problems, such as soreness, back pain, disc problems, osteoarthritis, degenerative joint disease, and minor sports injuries. In a complex case, you need everything that helps.

— Patricia Baley, DVM, a Traditional Chinese Veterinary Medicine practitioner in Houston, Texas

surrounding tissue, and can spread to other areas of the body. There are many kinds of cancer, and there is no single cause of this dreadful disease. Hereditary and environmental factors play big roles in the development of cancer in dogs.

Signs of cancer include abnormal swellings, sores that don't heal, unexplained weight loss, loss of appetite, bleeding or discharge from any body opening, offensive odor, difficulty eating or swallowing, hesitation to exercise or loss of stamina, persistent lameness or stiffness, or difficulty breathing, urinating, or defecating.

Osteosarcoma (OSA) is the most common malignant bone cancer in dogs, accounting for approximately 5 percent of all canine cancers. It usually develops below the elbow or near the knee, close to the growth plates. It sometimes spreads to other bones but typically metastasizes to the lungs, liver, and kidneys.

OSA can occur in any dog, but large and giant breeds have a higher risk. Dogs who weigh more than 80 pounds are sixty times more likely to develop osteosarcoma than dogs who weigh less than 75 pounds, and male dogs have a greater incidence of the disease than females do. The average age at diagnosis is seven to eight years old.

The symptoms of this cancer include lameness, swelling in the joint, and pain. A veterinarian can identify a tumor through X-rays or a biopsy and can recommend appropriate treatments, including chemotherapy and radiation treatments. A very aggressive cancer, OSA usually causes death within a few months or years of diagnosis. The median survival time for dogs treated with amputation plus chemotherapy is twelve months, with only 20 percent surviving two years.

Cataracts

Cataracts are one of the most common eye problems in dogs and the leading cause of blindness. A cataract is characterized by a white spot over the lens of the eye, impairing vision. The lens normally consists of two-thirds water and one-third protein. When the water/protein balance is disturbed, clumps of protein form, creating areas of cloudiness on the lens.

Trauma from an accident or injury can damage the lens and cause a cataract to develop, but the most common cataracts in Rottweilers are juvenile cataracts, which can be inherited or can result from a nutritional disorder during puppyhood. They may appear between eight weeks and twelve months of age, but cataracts can be detected between eight and twelve weeks of age 90 percent of the time. Juvenile cataracts can either remain insignificant and have no effect on a Rottweiler's vision or can cause early blindness.

Genetic cataracts usually affect both eyes and progress rapidly. When a puppy has inherited juvenile cataracts, it means that both parents are carriers. A vet can recognize mature cataracts by dilating the pupil and examining it with magnification and a strong light source, while a veterinary ophthalmologist can detect small cataracts with high-tech equipment.

There is no medical treatment available to prevent, reverse, or shrink cataracts, although a veterinary ophthalmologist can restore vision through an expensive surgical procedure. Veterinary researchers are developing a DNA test to detect whether a dog is a carrier. Responsible breeders have their dogs examined by a veterinary ophthalmologist and certified clear of cataracts annually before breeding them. Such dogs can receive a clearance from

Responsible breeders do their best to produce sound Rottweilers with healthy bones and joints.

the Canine Eye Registration Foundation (CERF); prospective owners should look for CERF certification on the parents of their new puppy.

Elbow Dysplasia

Elbow dysplasia refers to lameness in the front leg caused by one or more inherited defects. Three bones make up the elbow joint: the radius, the ulna, and the humerus. When the bones and cartilage of the elbow fail to fit together properly, it causes pain, inflammation, and eventually arthritis. This inherited condition is a complex trait, as both genes and the environment affect its development. A common problem in many large breeds, especially Rottweilers, elbow dysplasia primarily affects young, rapidly growing dogs.

One or more factors can be involved in elbow dysplasia:

- Ununited anconeal process (UAP), in which a piece of bone at the top of the ulna does not unite with the rest of the bone;
- Osteochondritis dissecans (OCD), in which the cartilage of the humerus develops a "flap";
- Fragmented coronoid process (FCP), in which a piece of the ulna's bone and cartilage is broken off;
- Elbow incongruity, in which the elbow joint does not fit together well and the cartilage wears out quickly.

A veterinarian can X-ray the elbow joint to diagnose UAP, FCP, and sometimes OCD, which is slightly trickier. A CT scan is usually more accurate than an X-ray. Surgery can help many dogs with elbow dysplasia; unfortunately, it may not remove arthritis that is already present in the joint. As a result, some dogs will still have stiffness or lameness after heavy exercise or during cold, damp weather. Regular low-impact exercise such as walking or swimming will help reduce pain later in life.

Hip Dysplasia

Hip dysplasia (HD) is the most common inherited orthopedic disease in dogs. It's also the most common cause of rear-end lameness in many large breeds, including Rottweilers. According to the Orthopedic Foundation for Animals' (OFA) website, of the 90,125 Rottweilers whose hips were X-rayed and results submitted, 20.3 percent were dysplastic and 8.1 percent were rated excellent. The breed ranks thirtieth (out of 157) in the list of breeds most at risk for HD. The actual number of dysplastic Rottweilers may be higher, as many dysplastic dogs are never X-rayed or do not have their radiographs sent to the OFA for evaluation.

Hip dysplasia is due to the abnormal development of the hip joint, meaning that the head of the thigh bone (the femur) doesn't fit tightly into the hip socket. This misalignment causes wear and tear on the hip joint, inflammation, pain, and lameness. Once this process begins, it's irreversible without medical treatment. Genetics contributes to the likelihood that a dog will inherit hip dysplasia from his parents, but even dogs from parents with good hips can develop this condition.

Severe cases of hip dysplasia are visible as early as four months of age, but it usually develops by the time a dog is nine to twelve months old. Outward signs include limping after exercise, a bunny-hop gait while running, difficulty jumping, and straining to rise after a nap.

Conscientious breeders will have their dogs' hips X-rayed and will only breed those who receive clearances for healthy hips. Puppies as young as four months old can have their hips X-rayed for a preliminary evaluation, but because some changes become visible as the hips grow and develop, a definitive evaluation cannot be made until a dog is two years old.

When the OFA reviews and evaluates hip X-rays, three independent veterinary radiologists classify the dog's hips in one of seven categories: excellent, good, fair, borderline and dysplastic (mild, moderate, and severe).

The PennHIP (University of Pennsylvania Hip Improvement Program) registry has a different way of assessing, measuring, and interpreting hip status. This method uses three separate radiographic views (distraction/compression), taken while the dog is sedated or under anesthesia. This method can be reliably performed on dogs as young as four months old. The evaluation report is based on a precise measurement of joint laxity—the primary cause of degenerative joint disease—rather than professional reviews.

For a puppy between four and five months of age who has been diagnosed with hip laxity, a surgical procedure called juvenile pubic symphysiodesis can be performed. The result of this surgery is that the hip sockets rotate into proper alignment over the femoral head.

Mild cases of hip dysplasia can be treated with nonsteroidal anti-inflammatory drugs; or over-the-counter drugs, such as buffered aspirin; or neutraceuticals (dietary supplements), such as glucosamine, chondroitin, and methylsulfonylmethane (MSM). These food supplements have a protective effect on cartilage (the connective tissue that helps forms joints) and can modify cartilage and bone metabolism.

Depending on your Rottweiler's age, condition and the severity of the degeneration in the joint, your veterinarian may recommend surgery. This can include a femoral head ostectomy (removal of the

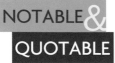

NOTABLE & QUOTABLE

Due to their large size, Rottweilers are prone to orthopedic problems. Keeping your Rottweiler at a healthy weight and in fit condition through moderate exercise can minimize these painful and aggravating problems.
— Debra Eldredge, DVM, a veterinarian in Vernon, New York

head and neck of the femur), triple pelvic ostectomy (modification of the hip socket; typically performed in young dogs), or a total hip replacement.

Regular low-impact exercise, such as swimming and walking, will prevent stiffness and help reduce pain. A Rottweiler should walk or run on surfaces with good traction and avoid slippery floors. Maintaining your Rottweiler at a normal weight will reduce the stress on his hip and leg joints.

Panosteitis

Panosteitis, or "pano," is a bone disease sometimes referred to as "growing pains." This is an inflammation of the bone found in large-boned, rapidly growing puppies. This is a painful problem that affects males more often than females.

In male Rottweilers, symptoms may appear between six and eighteen months of age. Symptoms in females will show up around the first heat cycle. Lameness that migrates from one leg to another can persist for as little as two to five months and as long as eighteen months. When sudden lameness occurs, it generally lasts from two to fourteen days and is not associated with any trauma or injury. Occasionally,

dogs with pano will have fevers, tonsillitis, or elevated white blood-cell counts.

The cause of pano is unknown. A bacterial infection was once suspected, but other theories purport that a virus may cause the disease. Other theories propose a connection to modified-live distemper vaccines or a genetic link; still others blame it on too much protein and fat in the diet.

In diagnosing pano, the veterinarian will look for shifting lameness, pain upon palpation of the bones, and signs of lethargy or anorexia. A series of X-rays can help provide a diagnosis. Pano does not respond well to antibiotics, although prescription painkillers or over-the-counter pain relievers, such as buffered aspirin may help.

After pano runs its course, there are few long-term side effects. If symptoms persist after eighteen months, the dog should be re-evaluated for the possibility of other medical issues.

Subvalvular Aortic Stenosis

The most common congenital heart disease in Rottweilers is aortic stenosis, also known as subvalvular aortic stenosis (SAS). This problem involves a narrowing just above or below the aortic valve, causing a partial obstruction of the blood flow from the left ventricle of the heart through the aortic valve and into the aorta. SAS can cause sudden death after regular exercise.

The abnormal formation of a ring of tissue causes the obstruction of blood flow. When a dog has SAS, the heart must pump blood harder because of the partial blockage to the dog's organs. The heart muscle builds up, causing an irregular heartbeat, reduced blood supply to the heart, congestive heart failure, or sudden death.

SAS develops during the first year of life. The veterinarian can detect it upon

Did You Know?

Dogs who spend much of their days on tile floors and backyard cement patios and don't get enough outdoor exercise may experience discomfort from arthritis and other forms of joint pain. Jumping on and off of furniture can exacerbate the same symptoms.

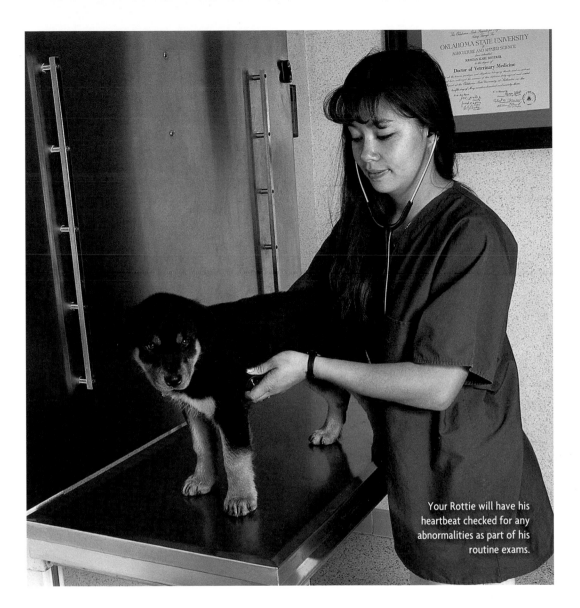

Your Rottie will have his heartbeat checked for any abnormalities as part of his routine exams.

examination by listening to the puppy's heart for signs of a heart murmur, which produces abnormal sounds when the heart beats. Sometimes murmurs disappear by the time the dog is around four months of age. If a murmur is still present after this time, the veterinarian may recommend referral to a canine cardiologist for further tests, including an echocardiogram, which measures blood flow.

If a dog is free of murmurs, he can receive a cardiac clearance from the Orthopedic Foundation for Animals. In mild cases, medication can be used to regulate the dog's heartbeat. Maintaining an affected dog at a healthy weight is important, as extra weight puts extra strain on the heart, and strenuous exercise should be avoided. Mild cases may not shorten a dog's life, and sometimes surgery can be effective, while severe cases of SAS can be fatal.

By only breeding Rottweilers who are free from SAS, members of the American Rottweiler Club hope to eliminate SAS from their breeding stock. The Rottweiler Health Foundation is sponsoring research to learn more about this disease. By collecting DNA samples from Rottweilers with an SAS diagnosis and those who have been proven clear, they hope to identify a gene for the disease.

INTERNAL PARASITES

The most common internal parasites are worms. They wreak havoc inside your pet, where you cannot see them, but they are easily preventable and usually can be treated. Worm infestation occurs in several ways, including through transmission from mother to puppy at birth, through the bites of insects that are carrying the parasite, or through contact with eggs or larvae in infected feces or in the environment.

Heartworms

Deadly internal parasites, heartworms are thin, extended worms that grow up to 12 inches long and live in a dog's heart and the surrounding blood vessels. When a mosquito carrying heartworm larvae bites a dog, the mosquito transmits the larvae to the dog. Once inside, the larvae spend several months maturing into adult heartworms, which reproduce and migrate to the heart, lungs, and circulatory system. Once found only in tropical climates, heartworm-laden mosquitoes now show up throughout the United States.

Symptoms of heartworm infestation include lethargy and abnormal breathing. Depending on how advanced the case is, heartworm can be treated, but the disease is often deadly, and the treatment very risky. Prevention is the best safeguard. Chewable tablets and topical preventives, administered once a month, are available through your veterinarian. Your Rottie will need a blood test to show that he is heartworm-free before preventive treatments can be given.

Hookworms

Hookworms are blood-sucking, thin worms about $1/8$-inch long that stick to the wall of the small intestine. Adult hookworms live and mate inside the dog, and their eggs are expelled through the dog's stool. The eggs hatch and mature in dirt. Although they prefer sandy soil, they may crawl into nearby grass. The larvae can live for up to two months, and a dog can become infested either by ingesting the larvae or through prolonged contact in which the larvae penetrate the dog's skin. Hookworms thrive in hot climates with high humidity.

Picking up pet waste promptly and washing concrete runs with a bleach solution helps prevent contamination. Heartworm preventives may be effective against hookworms, too.

Dogs of all ages are susceptible, but puppies are especially at risk. Symptoms in puppies include bloody to black tarlike diarrhea, resulting in anemia and sudden

Keep your yard clean so that a roll in the grass doesn't turn into an encounter with unwanted pests for your Rottie.

collapse and death. Adults usually develop mild diarrhea or vomiting.

Roundworms

The most common of all internal parasites, roundworms mainly affect puppies, but a Rottweiler of any age can acquire them. Roundworms resemble long strands of spaghetti, and their eggs are passed from mothers to their puppies in the womb or during nursing. An adult dog can contract roundworms by eating an infected small animal, such as a mouse or bird.

The eggs become larvae in the intestines and migrate to the liver and lungs. Roundworms interfere with food absorption, giving dogs a potbellied appearance, a dull coat, diarrhea, or mucus in the stool.

To rid a dog of roundworms, the Centers for Disease Control (CDC) recommend that breeders administer deworming treatments to all puppies and their mothers. If children accidentally ingest contaminated material, they are at risk. Heartworm preventives and many flea-control products include protection against roundworms.

Tapeworms

If a Rottweiler has tapeworms, it usually means that he has fleas. When a dog bites at and swallows a flea, he risks infecting himself with tapeworms if the flea is carrying tapeworm larvae. The larvae hatch in the dog's small intestine and anchor themselves to the intestinal lining.

These flat worms may reach 8 inches in length, but they contain many small segments, each about an eighth of an inch long. The segments break off and crawl out of the anus. Dried segments resemble grains of rice, which can stick to the hair around the dog's anal region and can show up in places that the dog frequents, such as on his bedding. When a dog scoots his rear along the ground, it could mean that tapeworm segments are irritating his skin.

Large numbers of tapeworms can cause liver damage, debilitation, and weight loss. Controlling fleas on the dog, inside the home, and in the yard will prevent tapeworms. Several types of treatments, in pill and injection form, are also available to treat tapeworm infections. A single dose can eliminate tapeworms.

Whipworms

Whipworms have a whiplike appearance and live in the cecum, which is where the small and large intestines meet. If your Rottweiler ingests food, water, or dirt contaminated with whipworm eggs, he's likely to become infected. Once the eggs are swallowed, they remain in the body for one to three months until they hatch and mature into adults. They burrow into the intestinal wall, where they thrive on the blood supply and lay eggs.

Mild cases don't exhibit symptoms, but if left untreated, whipworm infestation can become severe and cause bloody diarrhea that can be fatal, especially in puppies. Deworming medications can rid the dog of whipworms.

EXTERNAL PARASITES

External parasites include fleas, ticks, and mites. They live on your dog's skin and are the source of irritation and potential disease. It's easier to prevent these pests than it is to treat the problems they cause.

A close-up look at an engorged tick on a Rottweiler.

Fleas

Nothing annoys dogs more than fleas. Bites from these parasites cause skin irritation and unbearable itching. If your Rottweiler happens to be allergic to fleas, he'll scratch himself until patches of his coat fall out. Just a few fleas undermine a dog's natural immunity and can even cause tapeworm infestation.

It's much easier to prevent fleas than it is to get rid of them. Check your dog regularly for fleas by parting the hair on his abdomen and beneath his tail, as well as looking in the groin area.

Many flea-control products are available from your veterinarian, some in topical form and some in tablet form. Some prevent flea eggs from developing, while others kill adult fleas when they bite the dog.

Ticks

Ticks are hard-bodied parasites that are dangerous to animals and people alike. Ticks can transmit serious diseases, including Lyme disease, Rocky Mountain spotted fever, ehrlichiosis, and tick paralysis. Many flea preventives ward off ticks, too, but some over-the-counter products contain pesticides that can cause minor to serious adverse effects. Ask your veterinarian for advice on a safe tick preventive.

To detect ticks, feel through your dog's coat for bumps or anything that feels round and hard. Ticks can hide anywhere on your dog's body, but they particularly like to attach themselves behind the ears or on the chest, neck, back, and stomach. It may be difficut to spot a dark-colored tick on your Rottie's black coat, so use a flashlight or search for ticks outside in the sunlight.

Remove a tick as soon as you see it, being careful not to leave any parts of the tick still attached to your dog. Using tweezers, grab the tick firmly near its head and gently pull it straight out. Kill the tick by placing it into a jar filled with rubbing alcohol.

Mites

Mites resemble spiders and cause a skin disease called mange. Demodectic mange is caused by Demodex mites and is easily treatable; sarcoptic mange, or scabies, is caused by Sarcoptes mites and, while treatable, is more severe and is contagious to other dogs and to people.

Dogs can also be plagued by ear mites, which live on the surface of the skin of the ear and ear canal. From egg to adult, they live three weeks. If you notice your dog shaking and tilting his head or rubbing his ears on the ground, suspect ear mites.

Mite infestation isn't life threatening, but it's certainly irritating to the dog and can lead to infection. Intense scratching can cause raw patches of skin, and head shaking can trigger a hematoma, or blood blister, inside the ear flap.

Your veterinarian can detect the presence of mites by doing a skin scraping or by examining some of the dog's ear debris under a microscope. Once the vet has diagnosed the type of mite that is bothering your dog, he or she can prescribe an appropriate course of treatment.

Just one flea on a dog with a flea allergy can send him into a skin- and coat-chewing frenzy that leaves the area red, raw, and furless, possibly leading to a skin infection called a *hot spot* that may require veterinary attention.

it's a Fact

CHAPTER 8

FEEDING

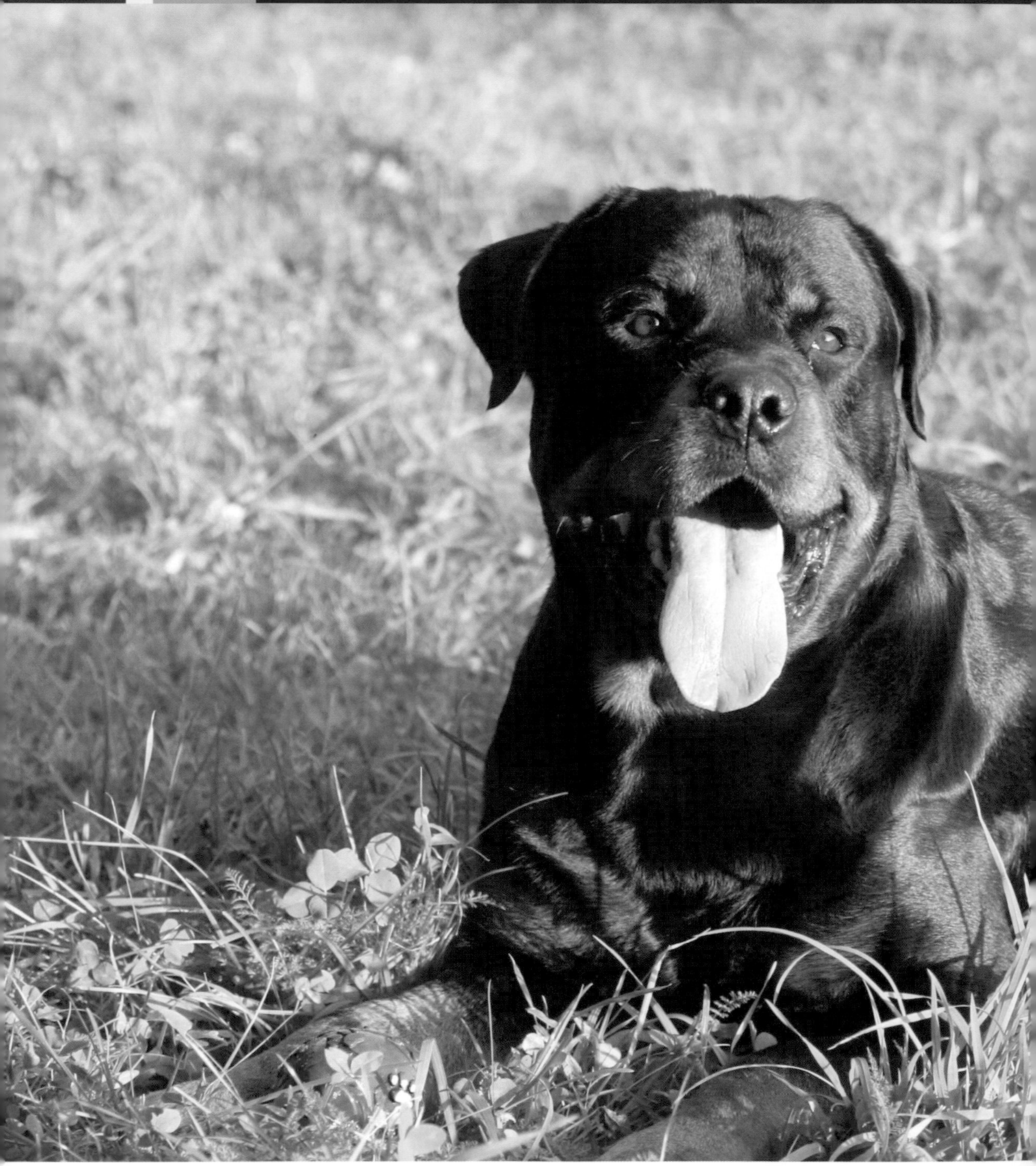

FOR LIFE

Throw a steak on the grill and watch your Rottweiler perform a happy dance and lick his lips like crazy when he gets a whiff of that glorious food. Rotties love their grub and will eat just about anything, so it's your task, as a dedicated Rottweiler owner, to give your dog the right foods, not just what he likes to eat. The Rottweiler is an incredible athlete who needs a high-quality diet to maintain his strong bones, muscular body, healthy skin and coat, stable temperament, and active mind.

By feeding your Rottie appetizing food made of wholesome ingredients, your dog receives optimum nutrition—carbohydrates, fats, proteins, minerals, vitamins, and water—in the proper balance. While foods with top-quality ingredients cost more, you'll make up for it in fewer visits to the veterinarian and a longer lifespan for your dog.

As in humans, overeating and underexercising accounts for obesity in pets. A dog is considered obese if he is 30 percent above his recommended weight. According to the Association for Pet Obesity Prevention, 45 percent of dogs in the United States fall into this category—that's 6.7 million dogs! Only 25 percent of these dogs' owners incorrectly consider their dogs' weight to be normal.

it's a **Fact**

BASIC TYPES OF FOOD

Today, more dog owners are concerned with their pets' health than ever before. As veterinary bills continue to rise, and people realize that they need to take better care of their pets, they're paying more attention to their dogs' diets. They're reading the labels and ingredients lists on dog-food packages and buying more natural products for their pets. They realize that the quality of what they put into their dogs' food bowls affects the quality of their dog's health.

As the popularity of natural and organic foods has increased for humans, so it has for our pets. A study showed that in 2009, pet owners in the United States bought 24 percent more natural and organic pet food than they had only two years earlier.

Conscientious Rottweiler breeders and owners agree that their dogs deserve to eat the most nutritious meals possible and to receive a diet that best matches the breed's physical requirements. Today, there are many ways to accomplish this.

Dry Food

What goes into those big bags of kibble, or dry dog food, that you see at pet-supply stores? The ingredients are mixed into a batter or dough and cooked under extreme pressure for a short period of time. The product is then formed into individual sizes and shapes and dried.

Dry food offers a variety of protein, carbohydrate, and supplement sources to choose from, and many brands have different formulas for puppies, adults, and senior dogs. Dry foods are available in large quantities, are easily stored, and don't need refrigeration. They're cost effective and convenient, as nothing seems easier than opening a bag and pouring some kibble into your dog's bowl.

Dry foods tend to be more energy-dense than canned or semi-moist foods. This means that your Rottweiler receives the same amount of energy from less volume of food.

Wet or Canned Food

Rottweilers like the strong aroma and the taste of canned food, but they have to eat a large quantity of it to feel satisfied, which isn't so healthy. Many canned foods contain a higher percentage of water than protein, are more expensive than dry food, and are higher in fat.

For a special treat or times when you need to coax your Rottweiler to eat a little something, giving him a few tablespoons of a healthy canned recipe might be just what the doctor ordered. When choosing a canned food, look for a recipe containing a

whole protein (meat, poultry, or fish as the first ingredient) and whole vegetables, not grain by-products. Always refrigerate or discard leftovers.

Semi-moist Food

Semi-moist food doesn't require refrigeration and usually comes packaged in single servings, which comes in handy if you travel with your dog. However, the food contains corn syrup to keep the ingredients from drying out, which tends to make dogs thirstier. There's also more sugar in semi-moist foods, which can lead to dental problems and obesity.

Semi-moist foods contain more water than dry food—15 to 30 percent more—making it a more expensive meal to feed because you have to feed more of it to satisfy your dog. For a Rottweiler, semi-moist food is best used as a special treat. If you need to watch your dog's caloric intake, the high amount of corn syrup makes this a poor choice.

Dehydrated Food

Dehydrated human-grade dog food provides a natural alternative to dry food. It appeals to owners who may not want to serve raw food or prepare meals at home. Dehydration preserves the nutrients that may be lost during the high-heat cook-ing and manufacturing process of kibble. Before serving dehydrated food to your dog, simply add water and mix.

Home-cooked Meals

If you would like to feed your dog meals that you make yourself, it's not as difficult as it may sound. You can prepare a balanced diet from the food that you make for yourself, but this doesn't mean table scraps. A home-cooked diet for a dog should not contain any cooked bones, fried food, or sauces.

A good home-cooked diet typically consists of a meat (protein) source, finely chopped or grated fresh fruits and vegetables, a carbohydrate source (preferably whole grain), a vitamin and mineral mix, and dietary fat. You can cook up a big batch that will last for three or four days, or you can freeze portions for future use. Consult your veterinarian for advice on proportions of each ingredient and what supplements to add.

NUTRITION 101

A balanced diet includes proteins, carbohydrates, fats, vitamins, minerals, and water in the right proportions. Read the labels on your dog-food packages to find the sources and percentages of the essential nutrients in the food.

NOTABLE & QUOTABLE

Giving your dog a quality, healthy diet helps avoid behavior issues. The food should also make your dog feel satisfied. Dog food with corn and fillers provides empty calories. A dog might be overweight, but he's still hungry. Hunger leads to food guarding, inability to focus on your cues, and hyperactivity.

— Stacy Alldredge, APDT, certified canine nutritionist and owner/trainer of Who's Walking Who in New York, New York

Protein

The most important nutrient in a dog's diet, protein comes from animal or plant sources and contains ten specific amino acids that dogs cannot produce on their own. Proteins are necessary for growth and development and aid the immune system. They produce hormones, build enzymes, regulate metabolism, repair damaged tissues, and strengthen hair and skin. Too little protein will cause loss of appetite, weight loss, poor coat, poor growth, and impaired reproductive ability.

Commercial dog food recipes usually

combine two or more protein sources to provide enough amino acids.

Carbohydrates

Starches, such as cereal grains, legumes, and certain starchy vegetables, are common carbohydrate sources in dog food. Carbohydrates provide energy when digested, but unused carbohydrates are stored in the body as converted fat and as glycogen in the muscles and liver.

Simple carbohydrates usually contain refined sugars and are quickly digested and absorbed by the body, while complex carbohydrates, such as whole grains, sustain energy for a longer period of time.

Try to avoid foods that contain carbohydrate sources with little nutritional value, such as rice flour, beet sugar, corn gluten meal, or brewer's rice.

Fats

Fats enhance flavor and provide energy more efficiently than carbohydrates do. For those Rottweilers who are picky eaters and need help maintaining a proper weight, the right amount and type of fat in the diet helps greatly. Fats provide more than twice the amount of calories as protein and carbohydrates, but they increase the palatability of food and aid in the absorption of vitamins, especially vitamins A, D, E, and K.

Working dogs who expend a high amount of energy need a higher fat content in their diets, but too much fat without enough activity adds extra pounds. Essential fatty acids are oils derived from plant and animal sources, and they promote healthy skin and coat. Too little fat in a dog's diet causes a dry coat, ear infections, weight loss, and slow healing of wounds.

Vitamins

Vitamins help maintain and strengthen the immune system, regulate the metabolism, and aid in digestion, reproduction, blood clotting, and the normal development of muscle, bone, skin, and hair. Contained in foods, they help process carbohydrates, proteins, and fats.

Fat-soluble vitamins include vitamins A, D, and E. Water-soluble vitamins include thiamin, riboflavin, niacin, pantothenic acid, pyridoxine, folic acid, biotin, vitamin B-12, vitamin C, and choline.

Quality commercial dog foods contain the necessary amount of vitamins, so if you feed a good dry or canned food, you won't need to add supplements. Check with your veterinarian if you're thinking of adding supplements, as excessive amounts of vitamins A and D can be harmful. Too much vitamin A can be toxic to the liver, and excess vitamin D can lead to kidney damage.

Minerals

Minerals are simple molecules that perform important functions in the body. They build bone and cartilage, regulate the functioning of nerves and muscles, produce hormones, and transport oxygen in the blood.

Quality commercial dog foods contain the right amounts of minerals, including microminerals, such as zinc, copper, manganese, iodine, and selenium; macrominerals, such as sulfur, calcium, phosphorus, and magnesium; and the electrolytes sodium, potassium, and chloride.

Water

Basic to all living things, water is the most important nutrient of all. Your dog needs to drink plain water for his optimal health. Water is responsible for transporting the

Rottie Birthday Biscuits

2 cups barley flour

1 cup rye flour

¼ cup chopped fresh or dried parsley

½ cup cooked ground turkey

½ cup low-sodium beef broth powder

½ cup unsweetened applesauce

½ cup fresh or frozen cranberries

1 cup water

Preheat oven to 350 degrees Fahrenheit. Grease two cookie sheets with a little butter or nonstick spray. Mix all ingredients together in a large bowl. The dough should be somewhat sticky. If it is too dry, add a little more water. Use a teaspoon to drop spoonfuls of dough onto greased cookie sheets. Make sure that all biscuits are about the same size so that they cook evenly. Bake for 10 to 15 minutes, or until biscuit bottoms are brown. Remove from oven and let cool completely. Store in an airtight container and refrigerate. For crunchier texture, turn off oven after biscuits are cooked and return cookie sheets to cooled oven for several hours or overnight.

Rottie Fruit Freeze-Ups

2 cups plain yogurt

½ cup sliced fresh strawberries

½ cup sliced banana

¼ cup blueberries

Mix all ingredients together in a bowl. Divide mixture into small paper cups. Freeze for 1 to 2 hours. To serve, pop frozen mixture out of cup or tear paper away. **Note:** serve these treats outdoors or in your Rottie's food bowl, as they melt as the dog eats them and will be messy.

A healthy diet builds a strong body and provides plenty of energy.

While household tap water may be safe to drink, it may contain high amounts of nitrates, iron, or magnesium, which can upset the balance in your dog's diet. Giving your dog filtered water to drink is a much healthier option.

Get in the habit of picking up your dog's water bowl every day and washing it thoroughly before refilling it. If you wouldn't drink out of it, chances are your dog won't want to either. Dirty water bowls harbor harmful organisms, and scratches in a plastic water bowl can trap bacteria. Stainless steel water bowls are recommended.

To encourage your Rottweiler to drink enough water throughout the day, keep his water cool in the warm/hot months and serve it at room temperature during cool or cold weather.

PROPER FOOD STORAGE

To make sure that dry dog food stays fresh and doesn't spoil, only buy as much as your dog will eat in a month. If food sits around too long, it can become stale or moldy and loses its flavor. Close the bag tightly with a bag clip or, better yet, store it in a container with a tight-fitting lid in a cool location out of your dog's reach. Keep in mind that many a smart Rottweiler has figured out how to get himself a snack by getting into his food.

Semi-moist food usually comes in single-serving pouches, and any unused canned food should be covered tightly, stored in the refrigerator, and used within a few days of opening. If you serve your dog home-cooked food and make a large batch for a few days' worth of meals, either freeze portions for future use or keep the food refrigerated and discard anything left over after a few days.

other nutrients, such as salt and electrolytes, throughout the body; lubricating tissues; and eliminating waste materials from the body.

Sixty percent of a dog's body weight is water, with the percentage even higher in puppies. A loss of only 10 percent jeopardizes your dog's health. The dark-colored Rottweiler heats up quickly in the sun and can become dehydrated if deprived of water. Your dog should drink two and half times more water than the daily amount of food he consumes and should drink even more during hot weather.

Remember to bring along water for your
Rottie wherever you go.

LABELS AND LIFE STAGES

Before buying commercial dog food, take a look at the label on the package—it should have the words "complete and balanced." These words mean that the recipe inside meets nutritional standards established by the American Association of Feed Control Officials (AAFCO) and based on regulations from the Food and Drug Administration (FDA), U.S. Department of Agriculture (USDA), and Federal Trade Commission (FTC) for the appropriate life stage (adult, senior, puppy, or pregnant female) of your dog.

The label lists a nutritional analysis with protein, fat, fiber, and moisture content, as well as the ingredients in descending order by weight. Quality dog foods contain whole ingredients rather than by-products. Less expensive foods use less expensive ingredients, requiring dogs to eat more volume of the cheaper food to obtain enough nutrition.

Puppy Diets

When you bring your puppy home from the breeder between eight and twelve weeks of age, he'll need to eat three or

Did You Know?

Leaving food always available for your Rottie promotes obesity and makes house-training far more difficult because puppies usually need to relieve themselves after eating. Regular meals help keep your puppy trim and enable both of you to adhere to a consistent potty schedule.

Foods to Avoid

Some foods, which people eat without a problem, can be deadly to dogs because of their different metabolism. While some of these items will cause mild digestive upsets, others can lead to severe illness or death.

Alcoholic beverages can cause intoxication, coma, and death.

Bones from fish, chicken, and meat can cause obstruction or laceration of the digestive system.

Chocolate, coffee, and tea contain theobromine, which causes vomiting and diarrhea and may be toxic to the heart.

Eggs (raw) may contain *Salmonella* bacteria and may decrease the absorption of biotin, a B vitamin, because of the presence of an enzyme called avidin in the whites.

Fat trimmings from meat can cause pancreatitis.

Grapes, raisins, and currants contain an unknown toxin that poses damages to the kidneys.

Hops cause panting, increased heart rate, elevated temperature, seizures, and death.

Macadamia nuts affect the digestive and nervous systems and muscles and cause vomiting, weakness, and lack of coordination.

Milk causes diarrhea.

Moldy or spoiled food contains toxins that produce vomiting and diarrhea.

Mushrooms affect many systems in the body, with the potential to cause shock and resultant death.

Onions can cause gastrointestinal distress and anemia.

Raisins can cause kidney failure when eaten in large amounts.

Salt in large quantities can lead to electrolyte imbalances.

Sugar leads to obesity, dental problems, and diabetes.

Yeast dough expands in the digestive system and causes obstruction.

Xylitol (artificial sweetener) causes hypoglycemia, which produces vomiting, weakness, and liver failure in high doses.

four times a day. He's active, and his body is growing quickly. Your Rottweiler needs more calories per pound as a puppy than he will as an adult. However, take special care not to feed your puppy too much, as bone problems are exacerbated when a puppy is overweight. Extra pounds put extra stress and strain on growing bones, joints, and ligaments.

If you feed a quality, well-balanced food, no supplements will be necessary, as everything is inside the bag. A diet for growing Rottie puppies should not contain more than 2 percent calcium. Too much calcium has been shown to influence skeletal deformities, including stunting of growth, osteochondritis dissecans (OCD), Wobbler syndrome, and hip and elbow dysplasia. Large-breed puppy formulas are available, but you may not need one for your Rottweiler if you choose a quality puppy food.

Adult Diets

Adult Rottweilers thrive when they eat regular meals at specific times every day. Avoid free-feeding, or leaving the food out all day and continually refilling the bowl. Most dogs will eat until they make themselves sick, or will just pick at their food. With free-feeding, you can never tell how much your dog is eating or if he has a change in appetite.

Most Rottweiler breeders recommend switching to a quality adult food when the pup is six months old. From six months of age and throughout adulthood, you should feed your Rottie twice a day.

Senior Diets

Every Rottweiler reaches senior status at a different age depending on the dog's individual genetics and overall lifestyle. Older Rottweilers are less active and generally require less food or a senior-formula food with not as many calories. Whether you choose to feed your mature Rottie a senior diet or keep him on his regular adult recipe depends on how active he is and whether he needs to lose weight.

Discuss your dog's diet with your veterinarian during his senior wellness exams. Your vet can advise you on your older dog's specific dietary needs, especially if there are any heath issues to consider.

TREATS

Treats are exactly that—special tidbits, not regular parts of your dog's diet. Feed goodies in moderation and read the labels. Treats should contain the same quality nutrition as your dog's regular food; there are many healthy types of treats available at pet-supply stores. Watch out for treats that contain artificial ingredients and are high in salt, protein, sugar, and calories.

Your dog will also appreciate cut-up pieces of fruits and vegetables as treats; these are full of fiber and nutirents. You can also bake your own dog biscuits and other healthy tidbits.

Did You Know?

Some commercial dog-food recipes contain yucca schidigera extract. This natural extract, made from the stem of the common desert plant, binds with ammonia compounds in the digestive tract and reduces urine and fecal odors. It's also known to have other benefits, including anti-inflammatory properties on tendons and joint cartilage.

IN BLACK

Just because your Rottweiler doesn't have a flowing mane doesn't mean that he can't benefit from some regular hands-on pampering. Like feeding your dog a nutritious diet, giving him enough exercise, and providing positive training, routine grooming helps keep him healthy.

Bathing and brushing helps maintain your Rottie's skin and coat in good condition and gives you the opportunity to check his body for the presence of any lumps, bumps, or scratches that may need medical attention. Giving your dog once-overs affords you the opportunity to spot fleas, ticks, or torn toenails; check his mouth for dental problems or swollen gums; and examine his ears for signs of infection.

If you begin these practices as soon as you bring your Rottie home, he'll start looking forward to the private time he shares with you. Regular grooming time turns a necessary chore into a fun way to spend one-on-one time with your Rottie and strengthen your relationship.

Did You Know? **All dogs shed. It's a natural part of the hair growth cycle.** Hair grows, dies, falls out, and grows again. Most Rottweilers grow new hair within about four months, depending on their overall health, their diet, and the weather. In colder climates, Rotties develop thicker coats and shed in the spring.

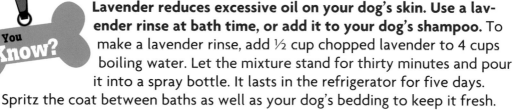

The Rottweiler's medium-length coat lies close to the body and is coarse textured.

has had some exercise or playtime so that he's more willing to settle down for you. Avoid handling your Rottie in a rough manner, as this only makes him fearful and resentful.

To help your Rottie relax during grooming sessions, make it a daily habit to slowly run your hands over your dog's entire body, including his mouth, ears, tummy, back, legs, and paws. Part of the reason a dog objects to grooming is that he's not accustomed to feeling human hands on his face, feet, and body. Once your Rottie becomes familiar with the process, and with some patience and practice on your part, grooming will become a snap.

It helps to establish a regular schedule for grooming so you're more likely to remember them. Brush your Rottie's teeth at the same time each day, brush him and trim his nails on the same day each week, and bathe your dog on the same date each month. Write dates and times on your calendar so you can keep track of them easily.

GROOMING SUPPLIES

Before beginning your grooming sessions, gather all of your tools and keep them within easy reach. You don't want to get your dog ready for grooming or have a wet dog in the tub and then have to leave him to grab a brush or a towel.

A Rottweiler doesn't need an extensive

To train your dog to enjoy the grooming process, start slow and don't try to introduce him to all of the grooming tasks at once. A puppy may not understand why you need him to stay in one spot for any length of time, and he may wiggle and fuss. When he's standing still, praise him and offer him a small food treat. It helps to have a grooming session after your dog

Did You Know?

Lavender reduces excessive oil on your dog's skin. Use a lavender rinse at bath time, or add it to your dog's shampoo. To make a lavender rinse, add ½ cup chopped lavender to 4 cups boiling water. Let the mixture stand for thirty minutes and pour it into a spray bottle. It lasts in the refrigerator for five days. Spritz the coat between baths as well as your dog's bedding to keep it fresh.

The Rottie's black coat glistens with good health when cared for properly.

collection of spa accessories, but the basics are a must:

- **Dog shampoo:** Use a shampoo specially formulated for dogs, as human shampoo has a higher pH level and can be harsh on a dog's coat. If your dog has skin problems, an oatmeal or hypoallergenic shampoo can be soothing.
- **Hand-held shower sprayer:** This is indispensable for rinsing your Rottie and brushing out the shampoo at the same time.
- **Nonslip rubber mat:** Gives your dog some traction in the tub so that he doesn't slip.
- **Peanut butter:** Helps keep your dog occupied during grooming.
- **Rubber grooming mitt:** Distributes shampoo evenly over the body and gives your Rottie a nice massage.
- **Towels:** Have a few thick, absorbent towels that are earmarked for your Rottie. In warm weather, you can towel-dry him after his bath to remove most of the moisture and then finish by letting him air-dry.
- **Pet hair dryer:** Comes in handy in cold weather; hand-held models quickly dry your dog. Do not use a human hair dryer,

as the temperature, even on a low setting, is too hot for a dog's skin and coat.

- **Rubber grooming mitt or rubber brush:** You can use the same rubber mitt that you use for bathing, or you can buy a brush that has rubber nubs instead of bristles. These tools remove dead hair while massaging your dog.
- **Soft slicker brush:** Any brush that's too abrasive will damage the skin and coat, so avoid a wire slicker.
- **Chamois cloth:** This is a great multi-purpose dog item. After brushing, a damp chamois helps smooth down the coat and picks up any loose hair. In hot weather, wet it to cool off your dog. Run a dry chamois over your dog's coat to add sheen, or use it after bathing to absorb water.
- **Canine toothbrush:** Some look like smaller versions of human toothbrushes, while others fit on your fingertip. Human toothbrushes are too big for a dog's mouth.
- **Canine toothpaste:** Specially formulated for dogs so that it doesn't need rinsing. Comes in a variety of flavors that are palatable to dogs. Do not use toothpaste for humans on your dog.
- **Cotton strips:** Long strips work well for cleaning ears. Don't use cotton swabs, cotton balls, or cotton pads, as these don't reach into the ear far enough.
- **Ear cleaning solution or sterile mineral oil:** Ask your veterinarian for a good ear-cleaning solution, or use mineral oil to help loosen earwax.
- **Large canine nail clippers (either guillotine or scissors type) or electric pet nail grinder:** Clippers get the job done faster, although a grinder lets you work with more precision and shorten the nail a little more.

it's a **Fact**

Like people, dogs have two sets of teeth in their lifetimes. The first set erupts through the gums when a puppy is three to four weeks old. These baby teeth fall out at about four months of age as the forty-two adult teeth, including the molars, start coming in.

Bathing your Rottweiler with a good oatmeal shampoo adds yumminess back to the skin and coat, as it stimulates the dog's natural oils. Use a rubber mitt when you work in the soap, and it's like a great massage. Your dog will love you for it, and he'll look forward to getting a bath.

—Wendy Booth, certification coordinator for the National Dog Groomers Association of America in Colorado Springs, Colorado

A tablespoon of finely chopped parsley added to your dog's diet freshens his breath, aids digestion, and helps maintain a good pH level throughout the body. Half a teaspoon of crumbled sage leaves mixed into your dog's food can help treat gingivitis.

- **Styptic pencil, styptic powder, or cornstarch:** Any of these will quickly stop the nail from bleeding if you accidentally nick the vein, called the quick, in the center of the nail.
- **Washcloths:** Useful during nail clipping. Hold the washcloth to your dog's nail if it bleeds a little; if bleeding a lot, use the cornstarch or styptic powder. Also useful for cleaning the eye area.

BATHING

A healthy Rottweiler coat is a clean coat. To keep your dog's skin and coat in the best condition, bathe him once a month, or more frequently if needed. Rottweilers who are exhibited in the show ring are bathed before every show—often every week or every other week—and their coats glisten and gleam with good health.

Regular hygiene keeps your Rottie's skin free of debris and odor.

Brush your dog before you give him a bath. This gets rid of excess hair so that it doesn't clog your drain. Bathe your dog in a warm, draft-free bathroom. If you feel like using the hose on your dog outside on a hot summer day, make sure that the water isn't too cold.

Before putting your dog in the tub or shower stall, place a nonslip mat in the bottom of it to prevent him from slipping. If your Rottie resists getting into the tub or standing still once inside, smear a little peanut butter on the side of the tub or at his eye level to distract him.

Start by wetting your Rottie down with the hand sprayer. Next, wipe around your dog's eyes with a washcloth or gauze pad and warm water. Start at the inside corners and gently wipe outward. Redness or swelling, excessive tearing, or discharge may be signs of an infection, and you should contact the veterinarian to examine your dog's eyes.

Apply a little bit of shampoo on the top of your Rottweiler's head and a few spots of shampoo down his back and along one of his sides. Work the shampoo into his coat with the grooming mitt, but don't get any soap into his eyes or ears. Next, turn your Rottie in the other direction and apply a little shampoo along his other

It's important to brush your dog's teeth every day and have them professionally cleaned once or twice a year. This helps prevent periodontal disease, which damages a dog's heart, liver, kidney, and lungs and also causes a heart infection called bacterial endocarditis. This threatens a dog's life and is very difficult to treat.

—Donn Griffith, DVM, a holistic veterinarian in Columbus, Ohio

Examine your Rottie after time spent outdoors for any dirt and debris that may be caught in the coat or footpads.

To remove skunk odor on your dog, combine 1 quart peroxide with ¼ cup baking soda and 2 tablespoons dishwashing liquid. Sponge the liquid onto your dog, allowing it to foam for two or three minutes before rinsing. Repeat until the odor dissipates. Dispose of leftover liquid, as it will explode if stored.

side; massage the soap into his coat.

Rinse your dog's entire body thoroughly, as any soap residue may cause itching and skin irritation. After you turn off the water, immediately drape a towel across your dog's body. This way, if he tries to shake the water off (as most dogs do), it won't splatter all over the bathroom.

Don't let your Rottie jump out of the tub until you give him the OK cue. Once he's out of the tub, towel-dry him if the weather is warm. If the weather is cool, finish drying with a pet hair dryer on a low or cool setting. Hold the dryer at least 6 inches away from the coat and keep moving the airflow around.

BRUSHING

A Rottweiler's coat may be tangle-free, but it still needs regular attention. The short double coat is composed of a coarse, straight, dense outer coat with a thick, downy undercoat. The undercoat is thicker on the neck and thighs. The ideal coat type for a working dog, the outer coat repels rain and snow and the undercoat helps insulate the dog.

To reduce shedding and to remove dust and debris from the coat, brush your Rottie once a week. A quick five-minute brushing keeps the coat glossy and removes the dead hair so that it's not shed around your house. The idea isn't to strip out the healthy hair—just the hair that's preparing to fall out. The rubber mitt or rubber brush collects the shedding hair all over the dog's body, while the soft slicker removes any dead hair in the fuzzy undercoat.

Using the rubber mitt or brush, start brushing your dog at the top of his head, then progress to around the ears and down the neck, chest, and front legs. In long circular strokes, brush from the back of the neck down the dog's back, toward the tail. Follow by brushing down both the sides and both back legs.

Using the soft slicker, brush first against the growth of the coat, then brush with the lie of the coat. This helps to reach each layer of hair and remove the dead undercoat. Finish by using a damp chamois to wipe down the entire coat.

NAIL CLIPPING

People pamper themselves with manicures and pedicures, and dogs' nails need attention, too. When nails are too long, they can tear and bleed, snag clothing, or scratch someone accidentally. Long nails can also make walking difficult for senior Rottweilers, who might be wobbly on their feet. If you can hear your Rottie's nails clicking on the floor when he walks, his nails are too long.

Contrary to what many people believe, not every dog wears his nails down on his own by running or walking on concrete. Some dogs' toenails grow faster than others no matter where the dogs play and exercise. Nail growth depends on many factors, including individual body chemistry, nutrition, and the shape of the nails.

Make trimming your dog's nails part

of your weekly grooming routine. Your Rottweiler should be accustomed to having his nails trimmed as soon as you bring him home. Don't plan on clipping all of his nails on the first try. Your dog may be resistant to the process, so start slowly with just one or two nails. When you decide that the session is over, wait until your dog is calm before quitting; otherwise, he'll think that if he makes enough of a fuss, you'll stop.

Put aside your fear of trimming a nail too short and making it bleed. Sooner or later, that may happen, but even experienced groomers occasionally clip a little too close. You can always ask your veterinarian or a professional groomer to show you how to trim nails properly before you try it at home.

Don't let the grinder intimidate you. It's a great tool once you learn how to use it because it enables you to see how close you're coming to the quick before you accidentally nick it. Initially keep the grinder on a low speed so that it doesn't vibrate on the nail too much. Once he tolerates the noise and the feeling of the grinder, you can slowly increase the speed.

Some people prefer to use clippers to trim off the ends of the nails and then use the grinder to finish. With nails that curve dangerously over the pads of the feet, the grinder enables you smooth out the under-surface so that the nails are flat enough to clip.

Before you start trimming his nails, let your Rottie sniff the clippers or the grinder. If you're using a grinder, start it on a low speed and turn it on and off a few times to accustom him to the noise. Give your dog a small treat so that he associates the noise with a reward.

To clip the nails on your Rottie's front feet, put him in a sitting position either on a raised surface, such as a grooming table, or on the floor with you sitting next to him. Lift and hold one foot just enough so that you can easily see his nails. For the back feet, it's easier to have your dog stand while you hold the leg backward.

Clip or grind one or two nails by taking off the tip where it curves slightly downward. Trim each toenail to within approximately 2 millimeters of the quick. After each nail, praise your dog and give him a small food reward. As he becomes more comfortable with the process, add a few more nails.

A Rottweiler's black nails can make it difficult to locate the quick. To help you do so, make a small cut and look underneath the cut edge of the nail. Repeat until you see a gray to pink oval starting to appear at the top of the cut surface of the nail; at this point, you've reached the quick and can stop trimming. If you accidentally nick the quick, apply some styptic powder to stop the bleeding; some dogs dislike the slight sting it causes, but it is effective in stopping the flow of blood.

Praise your Rottweiler continually, and give him a little food treat each time you trim a nail. If he gets too fidgety, stop the nail-trimming session and try again the next day. Struggling with your dog only makes the process more difficult.

Keep your Rottie's smile pearly white with regular dental care at home.

DENTAL CARE

Rottweilers, like all dogs, can suffer from dental disease. Brushing your dog's teeth daily will help eliminate tooth decay and bone loss. Because your dog isn't used to having someone's fingers in his mouth, you'll need to desensitize him to the experience. Start by putting some canine toothpaste on your fingers and letting him lick it off (it's specially formulated to dissolve in your dog's mouth). Repeat this over a few sessions, and then add some toothpaste to your Rottweiler's toothbrush and let him lick it off.

When he's accustomed to the toothbrush and toothpaste, it's time to start brushing. Place your hand beneath your dog's chin and show him the brush with the paste on it. When he starts to lick the paste off, put the brush in his mouth. For the first few sessions, you may be able to brush only one or two teeth. As your dog becomes more comfortable with the process, you can add a few more teeth each time you brush.

Brush the teeth in a circular motion with the brush at a 45-degree angle to the gum line. Work up to brushing the front, tops, and sides of each tooth, particularly the back teeth.

At each of your Rottweiler's yearly physical exams, your veterinarian will look at your dog's teeth and let you know when he needs a professional cleaning.

EAR CLEANING

Your Rottweiler's ears should be clean and odor-free. If you notice your dog shaking his head, scratching at his ears repeatedly, or rubbing his head on the ground, or if you detect a musty odor coming from the ears, he may have an ear infection and should have his ears checked by your veterinarian.

To clean your Rottie's ears at home, loosen the earwax by squirting some sterile mineral oil or medicated ear cleaner from your veterinarian into the dog's ear and then massaging the base of the ear a few times. Push a strip of cotton about half an inch into the ear canal and turn it to wipe out the oil, but do not probe farther into the ear canal. Repeat once or twice until the cotton comes out clean.

TEARING

The Rottweiler isn't a breed with excessive tearing problems, and the dark coat hides any tear staining. If your dog's eyes do tear, there are a few possible causes. Many veterinary ophthalmologists believe that the structure around the eye area plays a role in excessive tearing and that there may be a genetic connection.

Other medical reasons include a yeast infection or low-grade bacterial infection in the tear ducts, a blocked tear duct, or allergies. Sometimes a rampant ear infection or cutting adult teeth can be responsible for the eyes' tearing.

Some dog foods and treats can also play a significant role in muddying up a Rottweiler's eye area. Beet pulp, other additives, and food coloring are common culprits. Feeding a quality dry kibble with natural ingredients and no additives, preservatives, or food coloring keeps the eye area clean. Tap water with a high mineral content produces tear staining, too. Giving your dog purified or bottled water often helps.

If you decide to take your Rottweiler to a professional groomer, ask other dog owners or your veterinarian for the names of a few qualified groomers in your area. Call ahead and ask if the groomer or salon has any restrictions on the types of dogs they accept, and if the staff is comfortable working with a Rottweiler.

Ask to visit the facility to meet the staff and take a look around. Other than a little bit of flying hair, the shop should be clean, well lit, and should smell fresh. Individual cages should be large enough for each dog, and each dog should have fresh drinking water. Cats or other animals should be kept separate from the dogs. Equipment, such as grooming tables, scissors, combs, and brushes, should be cleaned and disinfected between dogs.

Watch how the groomer interacts with your dog. A good dog groomer should handle your dog gently, and your dog should like this person.

Ask the groomer the following questions:

1. How long have you been grooming dogs?
2. Are you certified by the National Dog Groomers Association of America or another professional organization?
3. How much is the grooming fee, and what services are included?
4. What types of products will you use on my Rottweiler?
5. How do you clip dogs' nails? Do you use an electric grinder or nail clippers?
6. Do you use a handheld dryer or a cage dryer? If a cage dryer, is someone always present to monitor the dog, or how frequently do you check on the dog?
7. Do you sedate dogs for grooming? If so, who does it and what type of training does he or she have?
8. Where will my dog be kept when he's not being groomed? Will he be taken outside on leash to go to the bathroom?
9. What happens if there's an emergency? Do you have a veterinarian on call or someone on your staff with first-aid training?
10. Do you maintain medical, vaccination, and grooming records?
11. How long does the appointment take, and what time do I need to pick up my dog?
12. What are your regular days and hours of operation?

Noble and highly intelligent, Rottweilers are capable of recognizing hundreds of words and following dozens of cues. When unsure about what to do, your Rottie will invent his own clever ways to take charge of a situation. By implementing positive training methods, including clicker training and luring, you can give your Rottie the opportunity to be successful at learning to follow your cues. Food, verbal praise, and well-deserved petting encourage your dog to repeat desirable acts. Who wouldn't want a reward for good behavior?

The training challenge with a Rottweiler lies in estimating how quickly he catches on. Smart dogs are easily bored with endless repetitious drills. Once a bright Rottie understands a concept, he will often try to create his own response to a cue purely for his own entertainment—but this doesn't

Did You Know?

Clicker training was originated through students of behaviorist B.F. Skinner, who first identified operant conditioning. They first used toy crickets to make the clicking sound after observing rats stop what they were doing when they heard the food container make the same sound, which indicated that food was coming. The students later used a clicker to train marine animals, such as whales and dolphins.

mean that you should ever relax the rules or reward a dog for undesirable behavior.

Teaching good behavior involves using the right training tools, such as a crate, gates, or other types of barriers, and a leash, to prevent your Rottweiler from making mistakes. Setting him up for success helps him understand how to make the right choices.

SOCIALIZATION

Once your Rottweiler has settled into your home and had his first trip to the vet, he's ready to make his grand entrance in the world. It's time for him to meet people and other dogs and to encounter new situations, and he needs to know how to develop positive relationships with others. All of these things, which are part of the socialization process, help him mature into a well-adjusted dog who's happy, confident, and a pleasure to be around. Your goal is to help your dog assume his role as a model canine citizen in the community.

Your Rottweiler received his early socialization from his breeder, and now it's up to you to continue the process. His early learning up to the age of twelve weeks forms his basic personality, so the lessons he learned from the breeder and from you during this time are critical. Starting between eight and ten weeks of age, puppies experience a fearful stage. During this short window of time, every encounter affects how your Rottie will cope with future events in his lifetime. Your puppy needs lots of interaction, affection, and handling from humans, as well as encounters with other dogs.

Proper socialization teaches dogs social and communication skills and how to judge the character of humans and other canines. To get started, clip on your Rottie's leash and take him everywhere that allows dogs—the noisier, the better. To help him become accustomed to a variety of sights and sounds, take him for walks in different neighborhoods, to garden centers, to home-improvement stores, to outdoor shopping centers, and through the car wash with you. Let him sniff the surroundings and walk on a variety of surfaces, such as grass, gravel, dirt, cement, and manhole covers. Let your Rottie climb a flight of stairs, ride in an elevator, and stroll across a bridge. Don't forget to always take plastic bags with you so that you can clean up and properly dispose of any mess that your dog leaves behind,

When you're out and about with your Rottie, you'll have many opportunities to introduce him to new people. Carry two types of dog treats with you—regular dog biscuits and flavorful cooked treats, such as bits of hot dogs or chicken strips, known as high-value treats. When you meet someone, ask if he or she would like to give your dog a biscuit and pet him. Each time this happens, your Rottie learns that strangers are not threatening and are fun to spend time with. If your dog seems unsure of a new person or situation, give him one of the high-value goodies to distract him. Let him meet a variety of folks—men, women, teenagers, senior citizens, skateboard riders, construction workers, bicyclists,

The best way to get your Rottweiler well socialized is to introduce him to different kinds of people and situations. Have him meet a man with a beard, take him to a dog-friendly restaurant, take him for a ride in the car. Go online to download a socialization checklist at **DogChannel.com/Club-Rottie.**

delivery personnel, people wearing hats… whoever you run into.

Enhance your puppy's natural curiosity around people by reacting in a positive way with something such as: "Wow! Isn't this a nice man?" This type of socialization with people should continue throughout your Rottie's first year, as many puppies undergo a second fear period between eight and nine months of age. Keep taking your puppy out of the house and introducing him to new experiences until he's at least eighteen months old, even longer if he needs more exposure.

Socialize your Rottie pup by introducing him to puppies his own age as well as to friendly adults. A good way to meet other puppies is to enroll in a puppy kindergarten class with your Rottie. Here, you'll encounter puppies and their owners in structured interaction led by a trainer who understands canine behavior. Ask friends with friendly adult dogs if you can introduce them to your pup in a neutral location (not the adult's home or yard).

Never put your Rottie puppy in scary or dangerous situations, as you'll do more harm than good to his self-confidence. You don't need to spend hours every day taking your puppy out; ten to twenty minutes at a time is plenty for a twelve-week-old puppy. As your Rottie grows, you can add more time to your outings.

Avoid taking your puppy to an off-lead dog park for socialization. At this location, you have no control over the other dogs, especially if they are dominant or too energetic.

CLICKER TRAINING

Clicker training, or operant conditioning, enables trainers to teach complex and difficult skills to their dogs without using force or punishment. Trainers capture the desired behavior with a cue word, such as "Yes!" or a clicking sound from a small training tool called a clicker. Rottweilers quickly respond to clicker training because they are intelligent and easily grasp the concept.

The clicker is a small plastic box that fits in the palm of your hand. It houses a metal strip that makes a sharp clicking sound when pushed and released. You use the sound of the clicker to mark a desirable behavior and follow the click immediately with a reward. Using a clicker allows for precise timing and clear communication about what specific behavior is being reinforced. Clickers are sold at most pet-supply stores.

Clicker training breaks a behavior into tiny steps and rewards the dog for accomplishing each step along the way to the goal behavior. For example, to teach your Rottie how to shake hands, start by clicking and giving your dog a treat if he simply raises his foot slightly off the ground. If you repeat this several times, he'll get the idea

it's a **Fact**

You can teach an old dog new tricks, especially if his diet includes the antioxidant compounds acetyl-L-carnitine and alpha lipoic acid. According to a study reported in the Federation of *American Societies for Experimental Biology Journal* by researchers from the Linus Pauling Institute (2007), these supplements significantly increase the ability to learn a new task.

that lifting his foot is what you want him to do. Next, stop reinforcing the slight paw raise and click and treat only when your Rottie raises his paw a little higher. The next step is to click and treat only when your dog lifts his paw and moves it closer to you. Keep working in small steps until your dog will put his paw into your open hand; once he does this several times, you can start introducing a verbal cue, such as "Shake."

Using this method takes time, patience, and practice. The trick of clicker training is timing. Click at the exact moment that your dog does what you want and quickly follow the clicking sound with a food treat.

Before you begin teaching any behaviors with the clicker, you must teach your Rottweiler to identify the clicking sound with a forthcoming reward; this is called "charging up" the clicker. Fill a small bowl with high-value special treats, such as cooked liver or chicken. These goodies should be cut up into small pieces so you don't upset the balance of your dog's daily diet. You want your dog to savor the aroma and flavor and pay close attention to you so he can receive another treat.

Hold the clicker in one hand and a treat in the other. Click the clicker. When your Rottie reacts to the sound by twitching his ears or turning his head in your direction,

A Rottie sits politely at his handler's left side, also known as the *heel* position, awaiting his next cue.

immediately give him the treat. Repeat the process of clicking and immediately treating several times. After a few times, your Rottie will look at the hand holding the treat as soon as he hears the click; this means that he understands that a treat is coming when he hears the click.

LURING

Luring is a positive training method that doesn't require any special equipment other than plenty of high-value treats or a favorite toy, which you will use to lure your Rottie into the desired position or behavior and then give him the reward for completing the action.

Luring works quickly because you don't need to wait for your dog to offer an action on his own. This method teaches dogs to focus on what you say and then react in a positive manner. The trick is to give the reward at the precise moment that your dog completes the desired behavior.

BASIC CUES

Every Rottweiler should know at least five basic behaviors: *sit*, *down*, *stay*, *come*, and *heel*. Not only are these behaviors the foundation for an obedient companion but they also are required if you want your Rottie to earn the American Kennel Club's Canine Good Citizen (CGC) title, which many therapy dog programs require. Numerous apartment- and home-rental companies throughout the United States require dogs to have CGC certification as a condition of signing a lease and moving in.

You can easily teach your dog the basics by using luring or clicker-training methods; both techniques are positive and effective. Choose the method that best suits you and your Rottweiler.

The *Sit* Cue

Knowledge of the *sit* cue proves invaluable in many instances. Teach your dog to sit before you feed him, before he goes out the door, before you throw a ball for him, and when he becomes overly exuberant. These actions keep you in charge and reinforce your dog's position as a family member who must abide by your rules. *Sit* is perhaps the easiest behavior for dogs to learn.

Teach your Rottweiler how to sit the day after bringing him home. Puppies are never too young and adults are never too old to learn this polite greeting. To teach *sit*:

1. Start with a treat in your hand and your Rottweiler standing directly in front of you.
2. Hold the treat over his nose and move it up and back over his head.
3. When he lifts his head to follow the treat with his eyes, his hips will drop into a sitting position.
4. As his back end hits the floor, give the verbal cue "Sit" and immediately give him the treat as a reward. Praise him in an upbeat tone of voice.

Precise timing is crucial. If your Rottie pops out of position before you have a chance to give him the treat and you treat him anyway, he'll think he's being rewarded for standing up.

The *Down* Cue

Once your dog learns how to sit, he can progress to learning the *down* cue. The *down* is a natural position for a dog, as it indicates to other dogs that he's feeling calm and means no harm. This is a great exercise to help an energetic Rottie relax and calm himself.

If you're taking your dog for a walk and meet a friend on the street, you may want to stop and say hi. In this instance, you can give your dog a down cue so that he'll relax while the two of you are talking and won't feel so antsy waiting for the walk to continue. For Rottie pups who are learning not to jump up on visitors to your home, remaining in the down position provides a calm way for him to greet guests.

To teach the *down*, have your Rottie sit. Hold a treat in front of his nose and gradually move it toward the ground in front of

With the proper training, your Rottweiler will be as well behaved as he is handsome. One certification that all dogs should receive is the American Kennel Club's Canine Good Citizen (CGC), which rewards dogs who demonstrate good manners. Go to **DogChannel.com/ Club-Rottie** and click on "Downloads" to learn about the ten exercises required for your dog to be a CGC.

his feet. If he moves his body all the way down, say "Down" and immediately follow the cue with praise and the treat.

Once the treat is on the ground, you may have to move it back toward you to encourage your Rottweiler to slide the front of his body forward and toward the floor to assume the correct *down* position.

The *Stay* Cue

After learning the *sit* and *down* cues, your Rottweiler is ready for the next step: learning to stay when you tell him to. Your dog will learn that when you say "Stay," it means for him to freeze in whatever position he's currently in, such as *sit* or *down*, until you give him another cue that it's okay to move.

The *stay* cue is probably one of the most practical and important cues that your Rottweiler will learn for both good behavior and safety. For example, if the door opens and your dog dashes out of the house, he could run into traffic and be hit by a car. Teaching him to stay could save his life.

Your Rottie will master three different aspects of the *stay*: duration (how long he must remain in position), distance (how far away you are from him), and distraction (what's happening around him).

Teach the *stay* with the following steps:

1. Start with your Rottie in a *sit* or a *down* position.
2. Say "Stay" and hold your open palm in front of his nose; this is the *stay* hand signal.
3. Immediately say "Good!" and give your dog a treat. If he doesn't move, say "Good!" again and give him another treat.
4. Wait another moment and say "OK." Ignore your Rottweiler for a few seconds until he gets up from the *sit* or *down* position.
5. Repeat, slowly lengthening the amount of time that your dog stays between the "Good" and the treat. Increase the amount of time in five-second intervals when your Rottie responds reliably.

If your dog gets up before you give the release cue ("OK"), immediately say something like "Oops!" and repeat the *sit* or *down* cue to get him back into position before you issue the *stay* cue again. Never punish your dog by hitting him, jerking on the leash, or yelling at him if he breaks the *stay* before you give the release cue. Your Rottie probably just hasn't grasped the lesson yet. Remember to give the release cue a moment or two after you give the treat—the lesson ends when you release him, not when he gets the reward.

To teach your Rottweiler to stay while you move away from him:

1. Put your dog in a *sit* or *down*.
2. Say "Stay" and give your dog the *stay* hand signal.

Did You Know? The American Veterinary Society of Animal Behavior believes that puppies should be exposed to as many new people, animals, stimuli, and environments as possible within the first three months of life. This should be accomplished without overstimulating puppies and causing excessive fear, withdrawal, or avoidance behavior, and before puppies are fully vaccinated.

The *stay* cue is taught with both a verbal cue and a hand signal.

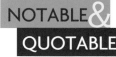
Clicker training is an excellent choice for all breeds, including Rottweilers. The concept of a training method that partners with the dog and encourages willing participation from the canine partner makes sense when working with a powerful dog. The clicker gives you a nonconfrontational approach to gentle and effective training for dogs of any size.

—Pat Miller, CPDT-KA, CDBC of Peaceable Paws in Fairplay, Maryland

When training your Rottweiler outdoors, keep some tasty treats in your pocket. Indoors, put tightly covered containers filled with treats out of your dog's reach in different rooms of the house so you can reward your dog instantly for following your cues no matter where you are.

3. Take one step back. Immediately say "Good!" and quickly step back to your dog and give him a treat. Wait another second and give the release cue.

4. Repeat the exercise several times, gradually increasing the number of steps you move away from your dog but always returning to give him a treat while he holds the *stay*.

Once your Rottie knows how to stay in quiet spots, practice in places with distractions. Have a friend come over to watch you practice, practice in public places, practice in areas where there are other dogs around. Keep his leash on at all times. Start slowly and progress in very small steps, as your dog will be distracted and initially will not be able to hold the stay for very long.

The *Come* Cue

Training your Rottie to come to you when you call him can save your dog's life. While some dogs never want to venture far out of your sight, others are inquisitive and don't mind wandering.

Teach your dog that coming to you when you call him is the best thing he can ever do. Never call your dog and reprimand him for coming. Always acknowledge his arrival with praise, affection, play, or treats, using a high-value treat every second or third time to keep him motivated. Make coming to you a positive experience every time, and you will encourage your Rottie to always want to come when you call.

To teach your dog to come:

1. Say your dog's name and give him a treat. Wait five minutes and repeat. Repeat several times, but wait until your dog isn't paying attention to you. If he turns to look at you when you say his name, say "Yes!" and give him a treat. Repeat this a few times, and then practice around several distractions.

2. Inside the house, say your Rottie's name along with "Come" and run away from him; he should run after you.

3. When your dog is close, immediately praise him and give him a treat. Repeat several times. Once he reliably responds,

NOTABLE & QUOTABLE

Rottweilers are like big sponges that soak up everything their owners want to teach them, but this doesn't happen overnight. They need to have drive and someone to spend a lot of time and patience training them. Providing positive training and socialization all pays off.

—Dede Brownstein, Rottweiler owner and American Rottweiler Club Volunteer of the Year from Albuquerque, New Mexico

Every time your Rottie comes to you when you call him, reward him with something that he enjoys, such as verbal praise, a treat, or some playtime with you.

clip his leash onto his collar and move the practice session outdoors.

4. Say his name, followed by "Come." When he turns and walks toward you, praise him and give him a treat. Practice until he responds reliably.

5. Use a longer leash and repeat the drill until he comes to you every time.

6. Practice around multiple distractions and in other locations on a 20- to 50-foot long line so you can gather it up and guide your Rottie to you if he decides that something else is more alluring than you are.

7. When he's rock-solid on the *come* cue on the long line, progress to off-leash practice in your fenced yard.

8. When your Rottie is reliable off-lead in your yard, move to another outdoor fenced-in location.

Exercising your dog off-leash without him running off takes a great deal of time and practice. For additional support, enroll in a good obedience class with your Rottie.

The *Heel* Cue

A dog who walks politely on the leash means everything when you have a dog who weighs 100 pounds. Your Rottweiler simply can't be permitted to yank you down the street.

To teach him to walk nicely:

1. Hold the leash in your left hand and ask your Rottie to sit at your left side.

Transfer the loop end of the leash to your right hand, keeping your left hand halfway down the leash.

2. Say "Heel" and move forward with your left leg first. Take three steps and stop. Tell your dog to sit and then praise him.

3. Once your Rottie walks three steps without pulling, add two more steps. Once he masters five steps, increase to ten. Keep increasing the length as he consistently walks politely at each distance.

4. If your dog insists on pulling ahead, simply stop. He'll soon realize that the walk continues only when he's next to you.

The *Leave It* Cue

Leave it is another very important lesson to teach your Rottweiler, as it could save him from ingesting something deadly. This cue will help your dog learn what he can and what he cannot put in his mouth.

After he learns what the *leave it* cue means, you can tell him to avoid items that might be dangerous, such as a sharp knife on the counter or a dead animal on the ground. This cue is also effective for deterring your Rottie from interacting with unfriendly dogs or people. The idea is to teach your Rottweiler that if he leaves something alone when you ask him to, he'll receive a bigger reward.

To teach *leave it*:

1. Have some treats in your pocket. Place a treat in your hand and let your Rottweiler see it.

2. Say "Leave it" and hold out your hand with the treat enclosed in your fist so that he can't get it. Let your dog sniff and lick your hand. Ignore his reaction.

3. After a few seconds, your Rottie will stop trying to get the treat and will move away from you.

4. As soon as he moves, say "Yes!" and immediately give him a treat from your pocket with your other hand. Repeat several times until he moves away from your closed hand when you say "Leave it."

5. Work up to walking your dog on the street and placing a treat along a short walking route. When you approach the designated treat, tell your dog to "Leave it" and keep walking. If he strains at the leash toward the tidbit, stop. Without letting him grab the food, say "Yes!" and give him a tasty treat from your pocket. Practice several times.

TRAINING TIPS

Training a Rottweiler isn't a mystery, although at times it seems magical when you can communicate a message to your dog and he understands you. Effective training consists of communication, motivation, and a few basic guidelines.

Be consistent. Once you establish the household rules, follow them every time. Don't let your dog sleep on the couch one time and tell him "Off" another time. It's confusing to him. He trusts that you mean what you say, and if he has to worry about how you will react to him every time he does something, he'll become skittish and unpredictable.

Be respectful. Rottweilers learn quickly. They are, after all, working dogs who naturally seek to accomplish goals on their terms. They resent being bullied. Treating your Rottweiler harshly will only make him ignore you or do the opposite of what you want. On the other hand, handling him with respect, fairness, and consistency inspires him to want to please you.

Have a plan. If you have a clear picture of exactly what you want your dog to do and have already worked out the steps for accomplishing your goal, you stand a better chance of having your dog comply. Use clear communication and rewards.

Provide an alternative. Merely stopping your Rottweiler from doing something you don't want him to do, such as jumping up on people, without giving him a positive alternative leaves him no choice but to find substitute behavior, such as barking at and body slamming your guests, on his own. Instead of simply telling your dog "No" when he jumps up, train him to sit politely in front of visitors to your home.

Manage behavior. Dogs will repeat behaviors that get a reaction from those around them. If your dog barks at you and you give him a treat, he'll think that all he has to do is make some noise and you'll hand over a goody. When you completely ignore his barking by not even looking his way, he'll eventually stop.

Provide regular exercise. A Rottweiler requires daily exercise. You'll avoid many common behavior issues when you give your dog ample opportunity to expend his energy in positive ways rather than in misbehavior.

Even the best dogs have some bad habits. If you are frustrated with a particular behavior that your Rottweiler exhibits, don't despair! Go online and join Club Rottie, where you can ask other Rottweiler owners for advice on dealing with excessive digging, stubbornness, house-training issues, and more. Log on to **DogChannel.com/Club-Rottie** and click on "Community."

JOIN OUR ONLINE
Club Rottie™

Bringing a new Rottweiler into your household will enrich your life and his. With an appropriate amount of attention and the right care, your dog will become a member of the family who you will cherish for his lifetime. Teaching your Rottie the rules and routines that you expect him to follow is an important part of welcoming him into your inner circle.

Disciplining your Rottie does not mean punishing him and using harsh methods, but rather introducing him to good manners and your expectations of how he should behave. Rottweilers need discipline in order to understand where they fit into the order of things.

Schedule a family meeting to discuss how your Rottweiler should behave. When everyone is on the same page and has the same expectations, the rules will be consistent. You won't have to worry about one person letting the dog sleep on the couch and someone else telling him to get off of the furniture.

Did You Know?

When you introduce a new adult dog into a household with another dog or dogs, it may take some time for his true personality to emerge. After a few weeks or months of initial calm, the new dog's confidence returns and he may begin challenging the resident dog(s) for social standing.

If your dog pulls while walking on the leash, stand still as soon as you feel the leash tighten. Continuing to walk with a tight leash only teaches your dog that pulling is acceptable. Stopping or even backing up right when the leash tightens lets your Rottie know that only walking without pulling will get the two of you moving forward again.

Discuss positive reinforcement—saying "Yes" more often than "No"—with your family. For example, house-training will be easier when you praise your Rottweiler every time he relieves himself outdoors rather than simply scolding him when he has accidents inside the house. This type of positive approach and consistency applies to all training.

Don't be afraid to use a time-out. When a puppy becomes overtired, he may misbehave. Biting hands, running amok throughout the house, or chewing on inappropriate items are all signs that a puppy needs a nap. Here's where giving him some private time in the crate provides an instant cure to a behavior problem.

The behavior issues discussed in this chapter are those that Rottweiler owners say they encounter most often. Sometimes these are the main reasons people decide to give up their dogs, which is a shame because with consistent training, these problem behaviors can be extinguished. Of course, every dog is different and every owner's perception of the severity of the problem is unique, but solving bad behavior helps you and your Rottie live a happier life together.

COUNTERCONDITIONING

While training by rewarding desirable behavior and ignoring undesirable behavior works well for most things that you'll teach your dog, this method isn't effective for behaviors based on strong emotions. Feelings such as fear, aggression, or a strong desire to chase small game require a program of counterconditioning and desensitization.

Counterconditioning means training a dog to display a behavior that is the opposite of his usual unacceptable response to a certain trigger. Desensitization involves gradually exposing the dog at a low intensity to a situation that typically produces an inappropriate reaction. You want the intensity to be so low that your dog does not react at all.

For example, if your dog becomes fearful and growls ferociously whenever he sees and hears a garbage truck rumbling down the street, you would work to desensitize him to garbage trucks so that his negative reaction becomes a positive one (counterconditioning). The first step is to find a garbage truck so far in the distance that the dog doesn't show any signs of fear. Next, gradually walk your dog closer to the truck, stopping frequently to feed your dog small pieces of highly flavorful treats. Continue doing this until you either approach the truck or the truck passes.

You'll need to repeat this desensitization process many times until your dog is conditioned not to react to the truck that once frightened him while gaining confidence and learning that the noisy vehicle isn't going to hurt him. Eventually, every time he sees a garbage truck, he'll actually become excited because he expects to receive a yummy treat. Food is such a wonderful motivator!

Walking your dog will be frustrating—or even downright impossible—with a Rottweiler who pulls on the leash.

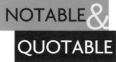
NOTABLE & QUOTABLE

Don't get locked into using just one training method. Every dog is different and may not respond the same to every situation, so you always need a Plan B. Never be afraid to try a variety of techniques, depending upon what your Rottie needs.
— *Frank Nelson, a member of the National Association of Dog Obedience Instructors and obedience trainer at Sanmann Kennels in Sellersville, Pennsylvania*

AGGRESSION

Mention that a particular breed is naturally aggressive, and right away people envision a snarling, biting dog. The truth is that aggression refers to a variety of behaviors that manifest based on a combination of the dog's target and the underlying trigger.

Aggression begins with a few warning signs from the dog and culminates in an attack. Watch a dog's body language for signs of aggression: a stiff, rigid body; a low, guttural growl; a lunge forward or a charge at someone; a nudge with the nose; a display of teeth; or a quick nip or bite that may or may not break the skin.

Often, owners don't observe or aren't aware of these warning signals and report that their dog suddenly jumped up to bite someone without warning. If you have an aggressive dog or worry he could become that way, evaluate the situations that may have instigated an incident. It helps to have an accurate description before you can obtain help for him.

Poorly socialized dogs or those who received little training may lack the experience or skills to react appropriately.

Providing basic training in a safe, controlled environment will improve any dog's behavior. In addition, obtaining help from a professional trainer with extensive experience in dog-to-human and dog-to-dog aggression is strongly recommended.

Dominant aggression is one of the many types of aggression. While many Rottweilers are content to let their owners be in charge, others think differently. A dominantly aggressive dog will consistently growl, snap, or bite when someone does something that he does not like. This isn't the same thing as an assertive or pushy dog who will generally listen to what his owner wants. The dominantly aggressive dog acts inappropriately in common situations. This canine is all about being in charge of the situation rather than deferring to his owner. It may begin as early as four to five months of age or around eighteen to twenty-four months of age.

The dog might display aggressive behavior over food, toys, and favorite sleeping areas. He may growl, snap at hands, or actually bite during nail-trimming, if his owner stares at him, or if he is reprimanded. At first, the dog will act aggressively only in certain situations, such as when his owner tries to take a toy away. Then it happens more frequently and in other situations, such as when his owner tells him to get off the bed or tries to pet the top of his head. It's not the situation that's the problem—it's the issue of who has the control.

Harsh methods, such as rolling the dog over, hanging him by the collar, or grabbing him by the back of the neck are ineffective and will only make the dog more aggressive. While intact males have a higher tendency toward aggressive

A Rottweiler who can see the sidewalk or street from his **yard** may be more likely **to** sound **the** alarm at everything that passes by.

behavior, neutering alone doesn't solve the problem.

Your veterinarian should examine your dog to rule out medical reasons for the aggressive behavior. Assistance from a professional trainer who has experience with this issue is necessary to break this vicious cycle; medication may be needed along with training. . Giving the aggressive dog more exercise may help reduce the frequency of incidents, too.

BARKING

Rottweilers aren't big barkers, but they will sound an alarm when they think they have good reason to do so, such as excitement during playtime, a response to the doorbell's ringing, and a greeting after you've been out of the house for a while. With enough socialization, your Rottie won't bark every time he hears a little noise or sees a new person.

For all dogs, barking is a normal form of canine communication, and they bark for many reasons. It's usually not a problem,

A 2009 study by the University of Pennsylvania, published in *Applied Animal Behavior Science*, showed that aggressive dogs trained with aggressive, confrontational, or aversive training techniques, such as being hit, stared at, growled at, or rolled onto their backs, continued their aggressive ways. Non-aversive training methods, such as exercise or rewards, were more successful in reducing or eliminating aggressive responses.

it's a
Fact

especially when you can quiet your dog with a single cue. When barking becomes excessive, it is irritating to you and to others. When neighbors don't like the noise, they may complain to animal-control officers that your dog is a nuisance, and this is the last thing you want to deal with.

Most Rotties will display territorial, alarm, and attention-seeking barking, but some may bark compulsively only when they hear other dogs barking, or when they're placed in frustrating situations. Occasionally, a dog may bark when experiencing pain or suffering from separation anxiety.

To decrease unwanted barking, determine why your dog feels the need to shout in the first place. Does he do it at a certain time of day? In response to a certain situation? At certain objects or sounds? At other dogs or at people? If you can pinpoint what triggers your Rottie's need for verbal expression, you may be able to reduce his exposure to that stimulus and, thus, decrease his barking.

To quiet a dog who reacts to strangers and barks to sound an alarm and guard his territory, limit his ability to see or hear people on the street. You may want to train him to associate strangers with a positive outcome, such as food and attention.

Do not try to soothe, coddle, or reassure a barking dog by saying "It's okay," as this only encourages him to bark because he thinks you are rewarding him for his barking. Your Rottie will view any type of verbal response from you as attention, so it's best to ignore his noise.

If your dog barks at people, other dogs, or vehicles during walks, distract him with small pieces of high-value treats before he begins to bark. Show him the treat and put it up to his mouth to nibble on while walking past a person, dog, or other trigger before he has a chance to bark. You can even give him the cue to sit as others pass. Always praise and reward your dog with treats when he chooses not to bark.

When returning home and your dog barks because he's excited to see you, keep your greetings low-key. Teach him to sit and stay when guests come to visit, as this gives him something else to do instead of bark. It takes time, patience, and persistence to stop your dog from doing too much barking, but the result is worth it.

BEGGING

You can't blame a Rottweiler for begging at the table. It only takes one tidbit from your dinner plate to convince him that the new hot spot in town is right next to you at the dinner table. At first, it may be cute to see your Rottweiler drooling in anticipation of getting a goody, but it gets irritating fast. A Rottie can get downright pushy. He might bump your legs, try to climb into your lap, and think nothing of leaping to snag a morsel before it hits the floor.

If you have a puppy, prevent the problem by never giving him a single bite. To stop a dog who has already picked up a begging habit, prevent his access to the table. Use a baby gate or his crate to keep him out of the kitchen or dining room when you're eating. Feed him his dinner or give him a food-stuffed toy or other safe chew object to occupy him. You want to teach him to do something else while you're eating, even if it's as simple as lying down in a designated area.

If it's not feasible to keep him out of the room, totally ignore him at mealtime, even if he barks for food. When your Rottie realizes that he won't be rewarded for hanging around the table, he'll lose interest and go to another room. Yelling at him only gives

It's hard to resist the
face of a beggar!

him the attention he's craving, and he'll continue begging.

Want to give your dog some healthy leftovers? Save them in the refrigerator and put them in your dog's bowl later. This way, he won't associate being fed "people food" with begging from the table.

CHEWING

It's normal for Rottie puppies to chew on objects as they discover the world. Chewing eases teething pain and relieves boredom, anxiety, or frustration; however, this behavior can become destructive and dangerous—even life threatening—to the dog if he swallows something harmful.

There are several reasons why dogs may chew. Those who suffer from separation anxiety may chew when they're left alone. If a dog is fed a calorie-restricted diet, chewing may be one way for him to find additional sources of nutrition. Then again, dogs may chew on objects just because it seems like fun at the time and it feels good.

For puppies who ruin possessions by gnawing and chomping, giving them plenty of safe toys to mouth will help protect your belongings from destruction. Observe the type of toys that your dog favors chewing on and give him a steady supply. Rotate his selection of toys every few days to maintain his interest in them.

Never give your Rottie cooked bones to chew on, as they can splinter and cause him serious injury. Edible bones may not be good choices either because dogs can choke on them, especially if they bite off and swallow large pieces. Forget about giving your puppy old socks or shoes to chew on, as he won't be able to tell the difference between these and your good shoes and socks.

Dog-proof by picking up anything you don't want your pup to get his paws and mouth on. If you see your dog chewing an unacceptable object, take it away from him and offer an appropriate choice.

Try spraying a safe chew deterrent on furniture legs. First, apply a small amount to a facial tissue and hold it gently to your Rottweiler's mouth to let him taste it. Chances are, he'll remember the awful taste when he smells it on your furniture and leave it alone.

Supervise your puppy at all times during waking hours until you feel confident that he's outgrown his need to chew. When you can't watch him, put him in a safe area, such as his crate.

COPROPHAGIA (STOOL EATING)

Some dogs will eat their own or another dog's feces (coprophagia), while others would never think of doing so. No one knows exactly why dogs do this, although there are some theories. Sometimes puppies will learn this behavior from their mother, who will clean up after her offspring to keep the nest area clean and predators away.

Veterinary researchers claim that diets with too little fiber and too much starch produce stools that are particularly appealing to dogs. They recommend feeding a more nutritious diet or adding digestive enzymes to the food. However, sometimes coprophagia develops into a compulsive disorder even after the diet improves.

There are some remedies to deter your Rottweiler from eating his own stool. Providing environmental enrichment, including toys and interactive games such as fetch, as well as physical exercise may help. Cleaning up feces in the yard immediately is always a good idea, especially if your Rottie

has developed this bad habit. In multiple-dog households, pick up after all of them several times a day.

Use the *leave it* cue whenever you accompany your Rottweiler outside to defecate; putting a muzzle on him before he goes outside is another option.

Sometimes adding deterrents, such as finely ground black pepper, crushed hot pepper, hot pepper sauce, or meat tenderizer, to your dog's food may convince him that feces taste terrible. This may take weeks or even months to be effective, and you'll need to restrict your Rottie's water intake for ten to twenty minutes after he eats a meal topped with such additives. Other food additives are available to change the taste of feces, but check with your veterinarian first. Often, such measures will not be necessary, as many puppies outgrow coprophagia on their own by the time they're six to eight months of age.

NOTABLE & QUOTABLE

Rottweilers are notorious chewers and can swallow anything that's small. Watch out for the squeaky noisemakers and eyes and noses on stuffed toys, and pick up socks and shoes. Your dog can choke on them or they can cause an obstruction and need to be surgically removed.

—Cathleen Rubens, a Rottweiler breeder and American Rottweiler Club member from Apex, North Carolina

A happily tired Rottweiler is usually a well-behaved Rottweiler!

DIGGING

You never have to teach a dog to dig. It's a natural instinct that many dogs relish. While Rotties in general aren't avid diggers, some have been known to excavate craters in their owners' yards. If having a well-manicured lawn is a priority, you shouldn't get a big dog like a Rottweiler. While you may designate one section of the yard for your Rottweiler to stretch his legs and potty in, he needs exercise and space to move around, so confining him to a small dog run is really out of the question.

Many dogs will dig when they're bored, and a Rottweiler will become bored quickly if left alone in a fenced-in yard for long periods. If a Rottie suffers from separation anxiety or dislikes being confined to the yard, he may dig in an attempt to find companionship or simply because he wants to get out of the yard. He may try to tunnel beneath the fence or gate if he smells small animals, such as moles or groundhogs, underground and want to reach them. Dogs also like to dig to bury special toys or just for pure entertainment.

At the very least, a dog may dig at the ground and circle several times before

it's a Fact

Dogs were the first waste-management workers, dating back 12,000 to 15,000 years. They ate garbage and human feces during early domestication to help keep areas around human settlements clean. A study of village dogs in Zimbabwe revealed that feces made up about 25 percent of the dogs' overall diet.

Most dogs will follow their noses wherever they may lead when it comes to finding a snack.

your Rottie has acceptable ways to burn off excess energy, he'll be less inclined to poke around at the ground.

To manage your dog's digging habit, try to figure out why he does it. In any case, provide your Rottweiler with plenty of exercise and playtime with you so that he stays active and feels as if he's performing important jobs. Getting your Rottie involved in an organized canine sport, such as agility or carting, may get his mind out of the dirt (read about dog sports and activities in chapter 12).

FOOD STEALING

What dog doesn't love free food? Most dogs love to eat, and they especially enjoy "people food." It's not surprising that a Rottweiler will counter-surf once he discovers that a snack is waiting for him. Leave a sandwich unattended on a high shelf, and an intelligent Rottie will probably climb on a chair to reach it, and he'll think nothing of stealing any tidbits within his grasp, such as from the coffee table or

lying down, as though he's trying to even out the earth to make a softer bed. Dogs will also turn over earth when they want to warm up or to cool off. In hot weather, your Rottweiler will appreciate having a shaded area to rest in and a plastic wading pool to splash around in when he's in the yard; these provisions can deter him from digging to find cooler ground. Giving him some food-dispensing toys that occupy him and exercise his brain will help to ward off boredom and prevent digging. If

Build a designated digging area for the Rottweiler who loves to excavate. Fill a small area with dirt and bury a few of your dog's favorite toys there. Take him to the spot and say "Dig." Use a shovel to move the dirt around near the toy. When he copies what you do and finds the toy, praise him and give him a treat. If you catch him digging elsewhere, immediately bring him to the approved digging area to teach him that this is the only spot where digging is permitted.

SMART TIP!

a child's hand. Also, if a dog is truly hungry and not getting enough calories, he's more likely to keep foraging.

To stop your Rottweiler from becoming a grub thief, simply don't leave any food out. Always put leftovers away in the refrigerator and install cabinet locks on the pantry. Never allow small children to walk around carrying food. In the process of grabbing food away from a child, your Rottweiler can accidentally nip the child's hand and cause injury.

JUMPING UP

Despite his size, a Rottweiler wants to jump up on people to say hello. Dogs sniff each other's faces when they see one another, so this is a normal greeting for them. If you don't want your Rottie to jump on you or your guests, only give him attention when his four feet are on the ground.

To eliminate your Rottie's jumping-up behavior, completely ignore him if he jumps up. Don't pet him, yell at him, or push him away, as any type of attention, positive or negative, is what he craves. Instead, cross your arms in front of your body and wait for your dog to stop jumping. When his four feet are on the floor, immediately praise and pet him. Remember to be consistent and resist the urge to indulge your jumping Rottweiler even once.

NIPPING

When puppies are about four weeks old, their baby teeth begin to erupt. To ease the pain of teething and to investigate their new environment, they will mouth and chew just about everything, including your hands and feet. These little choppers are sharp, and puppy nips hurt. Your Rottie pup needs to learn to curb his mouthy behavior and to stop nipping people.

Puppies learn bite inhibition, or the ability to control the force of their mouthing, during play with their siblings or other dogs. When a young dog nips a playmate too hard, the victim yelps and usually stops playing. The offender is surprised by the noise and also stops playing. Through repeated bites and play cessation, the offender learns the strength of his jaws.

If a puppy bites a human's hand during play, it usually means that he hasn't learned the sensitivity of human skin. To teach your Rottie not to nip, let him mouth your hands during play. Continue playing until he bites too hard. Immediately give a high-pitched yelp, as if you're hurt (and you may be). Let your hand go limp. When your puppy realizes that you've stopped playing, he'll stop mouthing.

If yelping doesn't work, try saying "Ouch!" in a low, reprimanding tone of voice. When your puppy stops biting and begins licking your hand, praise him and offer your hand again in play. If he bites

Did You Know?

Dogs have twenty-five times more nasal receptors for scent than humans do, and their nasal cavities are four times larger than those of humans. Able to detect odors at concentrations 100 million times lower than people can, dogs pick up the scents of other animals and determine their direction making it easy for them to go after game or to find and steal food.

Puppies learn about bite inhibition and the right way to interact with other canines through play with their mom and littermates.

To help with separation issues, keep your Rottweiler on a predictable schedule. Set regular times for morning rituals, including potty trips, exercise, a treat, a clean bowl of water, and the same verbal cue that you use each day as you're leaving the house. Establish a return ritual, such as a calm greeting followed by a walk, training, dinner, and playtime.

your hand too hard again, yelp. Repeat these steps a few times during the course of your play session as needed.

When yelping alone doesn't affect your dog's behavior, give him a time-out. The first time, move away from him for thirty seconds. If he starts mouthing again, leave the room or put him in his crate. Don't yell at him, as you don't want to use the crate for punishment; simply put him inside for a chance to calm down. Following a ten-minute time-out, resume play again and repeat the yelping and stopping.

After you teach your dog not to hurt your hand, give him a toy or chew bone when he tries to mouth your fingers or toes. If he attempts to mouth you when you pet him, distract him by giving him small treats from your other hand. This helps your dog become accustomed to being touched without mouthing.

WHINING

When dogs want attention or feel excited or anxious, they whine. If you leave the house, a dog will whine as a way of calling out to make sure that you haven't forgotten him. A dog with separation anxiety excels at whining, especially when he

senses that you're about to leave. This common form of canine vocal communication is one of the most irritating behaviors that dog owners endure.

Whining may also be a sign that your dog is in pain, so if your Rottie suddenly begins whining without a reason, take him to the veterinarian for an examination.

When a dog senses a threat or aggression coming his way, he will often try to appease the offender by whining. Appeasement whining is a normal canine behavior that is usually accompanied by holding the ears back, tucking the tail, and crouching or rolling over on the back. The dog will also avoid eye contact or will turn his body sideways, away from the threat. Building a dog's confidence by taking him to obedience classes that use positive reinforcement or getting involved in canine sports with him may reduce appeasement whining. Yelling at or intimidating a whiner only decreases his confidence and increases the frequency of appeasement whining.

Some dogs greet people by making high-pitched whimpering sounds; they become so excited that they lose control over their behavior. If your Rottweiler does this, keep from becoming too excited in the first place. Keep greetings low-key, short, and simple. Avoid flamboyant gestures and maintain a steady tone of voice. Wait to pet your Rottie until he's calm. Teach him an alternative to whining, such as sitting when greeting you or someone else. Try diverting a whiner's attention to a favorite toy or another activity. Your Rottweiler may whine less if he's concentrating on doing something more interesting. Telling your dog to be quiet usually doesn't work because he'll just continue whining a few minutes later.

For a Rottweiler whose owners are home most of the time and give him constant attention, being left behind when the owners walk out the door is often traumatic. A dog with separation anxiety may bark, whine, and cause destruction, especially around doors and windows. He pants, paces, drools, and urinates or defecates indoors, and he can become depressed.

Separation anxiety is the reason neighbors complain and valuable possessions are ruined. Leaving your dog in a crate, an exercise pen, or a dog-proof area where he can sleep and feel comfortable while you're gone will prevent him from causing injury to himself and damage to things in the household. Some dogs are comforted when they hear a familiar sound, such as the radio or television. Animal shelters report that dogs seem calmer when the sound of music wafts through the kennel areas.

Providing your dog with enough physical exercise before you leave the house helps tire him out; this way, he'll be more receptive to resting and settling down in his area with his toys when you leave. Taking your Rottie to training classes helps reduce separation issues, as training gives your dog something else to think about and builds his confidence.

To eliminate the problem of separation anxiety, teach your dog that nothing will happen to him in your absence. Start by leaving the dog for just a few minutes and gradually increase the amount of time that he is alone. For a Rottweiler who has already developed separation issues, you may need to set aside time for a systematic training program. Don't try to do this when you're running late and have to rush out the door.

For the first session, say something simple to your dog, such as "Take care" or "See ya later" in a low-key tone, without making a fuss that you are leaving. Say the same thing each time you leave, as this phrase helps your dog learn that you will be returning.

It also helps to give your Rottie a food treat, his favorite plaything, or a food-filled toy that makes him work to get the reward. Your nonchalant goodbye and the toy to occupy him help distract him from your departure and give him a positive experience as you're leaving.

Walk out the door, close it, and immediately come back. Repeat, adding a few more seconds each time. Expect to do this twenty or thirty times before you can add minutes. Keep adding more time until your Rottie barely responds when you return. If you open the door and he greets you in a frenzy, you may have to regress to leaving him alone for less time.

When you return, at first ignore your dog and walk away. Pet him and say hello when he is calm. The idea is to reinforce that being separated is no big deal. Your Rottweiler will soon realize that he will be just fine if you leave for a while.

SEPARATION ANXIETY

IN ACTION

Like all dogs and people, Rottweilers thrive when they get some form of exercise. Regular aerobic activity keeps the Rottie's strong, athletic body in good condition and helps provide intellectual stimulation to keep boredom at bay. As a working breed, the Rottweiler was originally bred to perform tough physical tasks—guarding and moving cattle, pulling carts, and defending territory.

If you don't live on a ranch where your Rottweiler protects your livestock, he will need a regular routine to keep fit. Besides, if you don't give a Rottie physical outlets for his energy, he'll find something to do on his own—and you may not like his choices.

Exercise and organized play help reduce or eliminate common behavior problems as well as help timid or fearful dogs build their confidence and establish trust in people. Regular activity keeps a dog's weight under control and can ease digestive issues and constipation.

Before beginning any exercise or dog-

Did You Know?

Rotties love to swim in lakes, but beware of blue-green algae, which resembles pond scum. This algae can produce a neurotoxin that can kill a dog in minutes. According to the Minnesota Pollution Control Agency, certain environmental conditions occurring late in summer can trigger a toxic overgrowth of algae in freshwater lakes and reservoirs.

Don't begin agility jumping or jogging with your Rottweiler until he's eighteen to twenty-four months of age, as his growth plates haven't closed before this time and can become damaged. It's fine if your dog runs around the yard or jumps up occasionally, but repetitive exercise of this type too early is a no-no.

sport program with your Rottie, ask your veterinarian to give him a complete checkup. Avoid overly strenuous exercise, such as jogging or jumping, with a dog younger than eighteen months of age. Such activity can be hard on the joints and bones, and Rottweilers are prone to certain orthopedic disorders, including cruciate ligament injuries and hip dysplasia.

There are many ways to exercise your dog, including organized canine sports. They require dedication and patience, but many Rottweilers and their owners enjoy the training and competition. Your dog can also get a lot of exercise just being active with you. Rotties are always up for a good time!

AGILITY

A popular and ever-growing canine sport, agility tests a dog's ability to maneuver up, over, around, and through obstacles on a course. Agility competitions are judged on speed and accuracy, and the excitement and fast pace keep you and your dog on your toes and thrill spectators. While the Rottweiler may not be the fastest breed in agility, he's a hard worker who definitely loves the challenge.

In agility, dogs scale an A-frame, climb up and over a dogwalk, and scoot through a tunnel or two. They wiggle around weave poles and perform several kinds of jumps, including through a tire. As if all of this wasn't enough, they are expected to balance on a see-saw and stop on command on a low table—all without going off course and without refusing to complete any obstacles.

Because dogs compete in agility without leashes, it's imperative that your Rottweiler is obedience-trained before beginning agility. He will need knowledge of the basic cues to follow your instructions and complete the course. Dogs can earn agility titles at varying levels of difficulty in competitions sanctioned by the American Kennel Club, United Kennel Club, United States Dog Agility Association, North American Dog Agility Council, and other organizations.

Agility gives you and your dog the opportunity to show off the Rottie's athleticism, intelligence, and versatility and let people see what a wonderful working breed the Rottweiler is.

BACKPACKING

Feel like hitting the open trail with your Rottie? If so, there are a few precautions that you need to take before setting off. Dogs younger than eighteen months should not participate in a strenuous hiking trip, as this can stress his growing joints. Take your Rottie to the veterinarian for a checkup before including him on your outdoor adventure. A dog who is even mildly dysplastic should not go for a long backpacking trip, as too much walking and climbing on rough terrain can weaken his hips further.

Before plotting your course, check that dogs are allowed on the trails, in the parks, and at the campgrounds that you plan to visit. Pack a bag for your Rottie according to the length of your trip. Rotties are capable of carrying their own backpacks, but you'll

Carting allows Rottweilers to explore the talents for which they were originally bred.

need to get your dog accustomed to the extra weight on his back for a few weeks before you leave. He can carry a load equal to one-quarter to one-third of his own weight.

Your Rottweiler's backpack should include a doggy first-aid kit with emergency medical supplies, a supply of his food and a food dish, a towel, a pad for him to sleep on, and a toy. You'll need to carry plenty of bottled water for him.

Your Rottweiler will need to be in great physical condition before a backpacking trip, which includes hiking and camping, so take him on shorter day hikes closer to home in preparation. Once you're underway, check your dog's feet every day to make sure that they aren't red or swollen and that there are no thorns or debris lodged in the foot pads or between the toes. Examine the rest of his body daily for foxtails or ticks and promptly remove them. Provide shade for your dog whenever possible and don't let him wander into the brush, where he can pick up oils from poison ivy or encounter snakes and other dangers.

CARTING

Historically, the "Butcher Dog of Rottweil" pulled carts of produce to market and guarded the money. Today, this mode of conveyance has become less of a necessity and more of a popular dog sport, although dog power does come in handy if your Rottie wants to help you haul gardening supplies.

The American Rottweiler Club (ARC) holds an annual carting test for Rotties who are one year of age or older. ARC carting titles are offered at three levels: the Carting

Started (CS) class, in which the handler leads the dog through the course on a lead; the Carting Intermediate (CI) class, in which the dog is off lead; and the Carting Excellent (CX) class, in which the handler sits in a sulky-type cart and drives the dog through the course.

The course is a minimum of 375 feet from start to finish and must include the following elements: left and right 90-degree turns, stop, fast, slow, back up, left and right 360-degree circles, serpentine or S-shaped turns with a minimum of five pylons, one distraction, and proceeding through a gate. A Rottweiler must also complete a group exercise by remaining in the down/stay position while hitched.

Start training your Rottie for carting on a solid nonslip surface, such as concrete or asphalt. Fit him properly with a quality adjustable harness designed for drafting. Other types of harnesses may injure your dog. Let your Rottweiler become accustomed to the harness before adding the cart. Put the harness on your dog several times while feeding and playing with him so that he associates wearing the harness with having fun.

Graduate to attaching the harness to traces (or two long leashes) and two milk jugs and walking in a straight line. Praise your dog and offer treats. As your Rottie's confidence grows, add the cart. Keep all of your training sessions short—about fifteen minutes maximum—and positive.

CANINE GOOD CITIZEN
The AKC created the Canine Good Citizen (CGC) program in 1989 as a way to encourage dogs to exhibit good manners in their homes and communities and to emphasize responsible behavior by dog owners.

Training your Rottweiler to pass the exercises of the CGC test paves the way to getting started in canine sports such as agility, obedience, and rally. CGC certification is a requirement for most therapy-dog programs and is sometimes required to rent a house or apartment with your Rottweiler.

You can take a class to prepare for the CGC test. You do not need to enroll in a class taught by a CGC evaluator, although only an AKC CGC evaluator can administer the test. You must sign the AKC's Responsible Dog Owners Pledge before taking the CGC test with your dog.

There are ten exercises that a dog must complete satisfactorily in order to earn CGC certification:

1. Accepting a friendly stranger
2. Sitting politely for petting
3. Appearance and grooming
4. Walking on a loose lead
5. Walking through a crowd
6. Sit and down on command and staying in place
7. Coming when called
8. Reacting to another dog
9. Reacting to distraction
10. Supervised separation

CONFORMATION (DOG SHOWS)
While the perfect Rottweiler in your eyes already rests beside you, conscientious Rottie breeders are always hoping to produce the ideal specimen of the breed. It's because of people's dedication to the breed that the Rottweiler has continued for generations.

Dog shows were created to evaluate breeding stock, as only the best were chosen to perpetuate the breed. Today, the process at dog shows is pretty much the same: a judge evaluates dogs of both sexes to see how closely they exemplify the qualities set forth in the breed standard.

Dogs in competition cannot be spayed or neutered, and they must be registered with the hosting organization (e.g., AKC, UKC, Canadian Kennel Club) to participate in conformation shows.

If you're interested in showing your Rottweiler, ask your breeder to honestly evaluate your dog's show potential. The competition inside the show ring is stiff, and the dogs who come closest to meeting the breed standard are the ones who are successful. You'll also need to learn how to show your dog; it's a good idea to take a handling class before entering a show so that you and your Rottie both have an idea of what to do in the ring.

To evaluate your Rottweiler, the judge will feel his body, look inside his mouth, make sure that he (or she) is sexually intact, and watch your dog's gait from the side and coming and going. While Rottweilers are permitted to act aloof when the judge examines them, no sign of aggression is tolerated. Dogs must have stellar temperaments to be show dogs. You won't need any special equipment other than a thin leash and collar, a crate to transport your dog in the car, some high-value food treats, fresh water, and some basic grooming supplies.

At many shows, males are shown separately from females, and the competing dogs are divided into separate classes for puppies, adolescent dogs, and adults. Winning dogs earn points toward their championship titles.

DANCING WITH DOGS (CANINE FREESTYLE)

If you and your Rottweiler love dancing to music around the house, canine freestyle may be the perfect sport for you. Moving without leashes, dogs perform rhythmical, choreographed routines set to music

Competitive sports, such as obedience, allow you to bond with your Rottie and meet other owners who are passionate about training.

alongside their owners. Performances are judged on technical and artistic merit, including level of difficulty and precision of movement, attitude of the dog, interpretation of the music, and synchronization to the music.

Dogs must be able to follow cues given by their handlers, and some advanced training skills are required for top-level competition. These include heeling on both sides of the handler, walking backward, pivoting, and side-stepping. For dogs to earn high scores they must really enjoy performing. Dogs and handlers often wear coordinating costumes to match the theme of their music.

While Rottweilers may not be the most agile of canine performers, they certainly excel in showing off the bond they share with their owners. Canine freestyle training can pay off in other ways, too; for example,

Playing fetch with a stick is dangerous for your dog. A stick can injure your Rottie when he runs to retrieve it. Splinters can enter your dog's mouth, nose, or eyes, causing infection and injury. Use sturdy rubber balls or fabric flying discs instead.

if you participate in therapy-dog activities, performing a dance routine with your Rottweiler is always a crowd pleaser.

The Canine Freestyle Federation, Musical Dog Sports Association, and World Canine Freestyle Organization are the major organizations that sponsor freestyle events. If you're interested, attend an event without your dog to see what it entails and to decide if you and your Rottweiler would like to get involved.

FLYBALL

Flyball is a fast-paced relay sport that will keep you and your Rottweiler's hearts racing. For dogs who go nuts after tennis balls, this sport showcases their speed and athleticism.

This is a team sport, with each team made up of four dogs and their handlers. Each dog runs down a lane and jumps over four hurdles spaced approximately 10 feet apart. About 15 feet beyond the last hurdle is a spring-loaded box containing a tennis ball. The dog steps on a pedal on the box to release the ball, catches the ball in mid-air, and races back over the four hurdles to the start line, at which point the next dog takes his turn.

The first team to have all four dogs run without committing any errors wins the heat. When a dog skips a hurdle or doesn't

retrieve the ball, he must repeat his turn.

Flyball always draws a crowd of fans who love to cheer and yell, which heightens the dogs' excitement. It's hard to decide who has more fun in this sport—you, your dog, or the spectators.

HERDING

With his background as a working cattle herder and drover dog extraordinaire, Rottweilers may participate in AKC herding tests and trials. These events are staged simulations of how dogs move livestock, designed to demonstrate the dogs' ability to perform their original tasks.

Herding events provide a standardized way for owners to measure their dogs' natural herding abilities and training. AKC herding tests are noncompetitive events for dogs with no prior herding experience. Dogs can earn certifications, proving that they show herding instinct, are under basic control, and work together with their handlers. Herding trials are competitive events that test dogs with experience.

OBEDIENCE

Obedience trials measure how proficiently a dog has been trained to execute a variety of tasks on cue. Obedience exercises include basic skills, such as heel, sit, stay, down, being examined by the judge, and coming when called, and progress to more complicated skills at intermediate and advanced levels.

There's only one chance to complete each task, and precision counts. All dogs begin with a perfect score of 200, and points are deducted for errors. In AKC obedience, dogs work to complete qualifying "legs" toward titles at each level of competition. The Companion Dog (CD) title is available at the Novice level; the Companion Dog

Owners and Rottweilers can practice many obedience exercises, such as retrieving a dumbbell, in their own backyards.

Excellent (CDX) title at the Open level; and the Utility Dog (UD) and Utility Dog Excellent (UDX) titles at the Utility level. The top-scoring dog at an obedience trial receives the prestigious High in Trial (HIT) designation. The UKC holds its own obedience trials and offers its own titles.

When given the chance, Rottweilers excel at obedience. Their keen sense and intelligence enable them to grasp concepts quickly and work to completion. While you may not want to compete in formal obedience and might not need your Rottie to follow your cues as precisely at home as he would need to in the obedience ring, taking your Rottie to competitive obedience training classes will sharpen both of your skills.

RALLY

AKC rally is a new dog sport that any trained dog, purebred or mixed breed, can compete in. Rally gives dog-and-handler teams the chance to complete a series of exercises, laid out as a course of ten to twenty designated stations, at their own pace. At each station, a sign indicates what skill the team must perform before moving on to the next station.

Competing in rally is all about the teamwork between dog and handler, but this is a less formal event than traditional obedience. For example, perfect heel position is not required in rally, although the dog must remain on the handler's left side. Communication from handler to dog is unrestricted in rally. Multiple directions and/or hand signals are permitted, although harsh

SMART TIP! When driving your Rottie to outdoor activities, don't let him jump in or out of the car, as this can cause serious injury to his joints. Use a dog ramp or teach him a feet up cue. When he puts his feet up on the car seat, praise and reward him and then lift his rear legs up.

verbal commands or intimidating gestures are penalized.

The three levels of rally competition are Novice, Advanced, and Excellent, and all exercises are done on leash. While each performance is timed, the times are only considered if two dogs earn the same score. All teams begin with a perfect score of 100, and a score of at least 70 points is a qualifying score. After three qualifying scores at a given level, dogs can earn the title available at that level: Rally Novice (RN), Rally Advanced (RA), and Rally Excellent (RE). To earn a Rally Advanced Excellent (RAE), teams must qualify ten times in a combination of Advanced and Excellent classes.

SKIJORING

For an athletic Rottweiler, running in the snow and pulling his owner on skis behind him brings great joy. The picture of a black-and-rust Rottie having the time of his life against a backdrop of pure white snow seems idyllic.

Skijoring began in the mid-1950s in the Scandinavian countries as a way to travel during the long winters. It is an individual sport, although competitive skijoring competitions are held in a few states in the United States. On an individual level, it's you and your Rottweiler going out for a day of play in the snow. What could be better?

Any dog heavier than 30 pounds can participate in skijoring—all you need is a pair of cross-country skis and a harness for your dog. Skijoring is easy to learn, but first you'll need to learn how to ski cross-country. Your Rottweiler must be comfortable wearing a harness, know basic obedience cues, and know how to pull. Rottweilers naturally love to pull, so if your dog has had carting instruction, skijoring should be very easy for him.

THERAPY ACTIVITIES

The sight of a big, strong Rottweiler cuddling against a bedridden child or adult is heartwarming. Much has been learned about the incredible healing power of animals, and the Rottweiler seems tailor-made to bring comfort to anyone in need.

A therapy dog visits people of all ages in a variety of therapeutic settings, including schools, rehabilitation facilities, disaster centers, hospitals, and long-term care centers, to provide snuggles and companionship. Animal-assisted therapy (AAT) uses dogs as part of a patient's rehabilitation. The health-care professional designs a treatment plan that incorporates canine interactions to improve the patient's physical or emotional function. Patients often show vast improvement once they begin working with dogs.

With his soft, dark brown eyes and stubby wagging tail, a Rottweiler knows when it's time to be calm and gentle, but all therapy dogs must be trained. Even the sweetest Rottweiler can be intimidating to someone who is unfamiliar with the breed's true nature. Therapy dogs must have the physical and mental strength to cope with strange noises and smells, odd distractions, clumsy petting, and often confusing behavior from patients. They should be people-friendly,

NOTABLE & QUOTABLE

I started training my eight-week-old puppy, D'Kota, for therapy work by socializing her. By four months of age, she had met over 150 people. The day at the Ronald McDonald House when a child with cerebral palsy climbed out of bed for the first time and held onto D'Kota's coat to walk to physical therapy made it worthwhile.

— *Dr. Tommy Caisango, child psychologist and pet therapy chairperson for the American Rottweiler Club of America from Melbourne, Florida*

enjoy going to new places, and be happy and calm in new situations. They must be able to take treats or toys from a person gently, without nipping hands. Mature dogs tend to make the best therapy dogs, as they generally are less excitable and more relaxed.

If you're interested in getting involved in therapy work with your Rottweiler, start by earning CGC certification and then becoming certified as a therapy team by a reputable therapy dog organization. Delta Society (www.deltasociety.org) and Therapy Dogs International (www.tdi-dog.org) are two organizations that screen volunteers, evaluate dogs, and register therapy dog teams in the United States and Canada. The best way to begin is to contact a local canine therapy group or a local affiliate of a national organization to learn about the group's therapy activities and requirements for volunteers.

TRACKING

Tracking events, in which dogs follow a scented track and locate articles left by a tracklayer, test a Rottweiler's ability to recognize and track human scent over different terrains and with climatic changes. While Rotties aren't used by search and rescue agencies extensively, there's no reason why they shouldn't be. In tracking tests, Rotties excel with their intelligence and high level of scenting ability.

The AKC offers three different tracking titles: Tracking Dog (TD), Tracking Dog Excellent (TDX), and Variable Surface Tracking (VST). When a Rottie completes all three tracking titles, he receives the title of Champion Tracker (CT).

To earn the TD title, dogs must follow a track of 440 to 500 yards, with three to five changes of direction that has been aged from thirty minutes to two hours. The TDX and VST titles are more difficult to earn, as the tracks are more complex.

Most Rottweilers require very little training before competing in tracking. This breed is eager to work and enjoys being outdoors.

WEIGHT PULLING

A dog capable of hauling a cart can also compete in weight pulling. Muscular Rottweilers are naturals for this sport, as they love to work and they love to pull. Weight-pull fans enjoy the excitement as they root for their favorite dogs.

The competition involves harnessing a dog to a sled or cart loaded with weights to see and how much weight can be moved how far in a specified amount of time. Dogs are judged on the amount of weight that they pull in relation to their body weight. The harnesses are specially designed to keep pressure off of the dogs' necks and prevent injury.

During successive rounds, dogs pull several times. Weights are added after each successful round. The dogs are given a short rest between pulls, and they must pull each load about 16 feet within sixty seconds for the pull to count. The weight is gradually increased until only one dog remains. Contests are held on a variety of surfaces—grass, dirt, snow, or rail tracks— depending upon where the competitions are located.

In events sanctioned by the International Weight Pull Association (www.iwpa.net), dogs must be between the ages of one year and twelve years. They compete in eight weight classes and must be conditioned and trained to prevent injuries. The United National Weight Pull Association (www. unwpa.com) is a coalition of clubs and individuals dedicated to this sport. The UKC also sponsors its own weight pull events.

Swimming is great exercise for your Rottweiler and is enjoyed by many dogs who are introduced to water properly.

NOTABLE & QUOTABLE

It was easy to train our first Rottie to "shut the door." Whenever I came home with groceries, I told Brandy to shut the door, and she would jump up on the handle and push the door closed. She loved doing it and acted so important.
—Gwen Chaney, past president of the American Rottweiler Club
from Indianapolis, Indiana

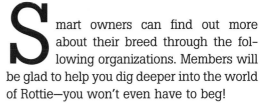

Smart owners can find out more about their breed through the following organizations. Members will be glad to help you dig deeper into the world of Rottie—you won't even have to beg!

Academy of Veterinary Homeopathy: The AVH's membership of veterinarians and veterinary students is devoted to furthering education and research in veterinary homeopathy. The organization also certifies veterinary homeopaths. www.theavh.org

American Animal Hospital Association: The AAHA accredits small animal hospitals throughout the United States and Canada. www.healthypet.com

American Dog Owners Association: A nationwide group of dog owners and fanciers who promote responsible ownership and owners' rights. www.adoa.org

American Holistic Veterinary Medical Association: This professional organization for holistic veterinarians promotes alternative health-care techniques and supports research in the field. www.ahvma.org

American Humane Association: This nonprofit organization founded in 1877 is dedicated to protecting children and animals. www.americanhumane.org

American Kennel Club: Founded in 1884, the AKC is America's oldest purebred dog registry. It governs conformation, companion, and performance events and promotes responsible dog ownership. www.akc.org

American Kennel Club Canine Health Foundation: This foundation is the largest nonprofit funder of exclusively canine research in the world. www.akcchf.org

American Rottweiler Club: This is the national AKC parent club for the Rottweiler, dedicated to responsible breeding and ownership, advancement of the breed, public education, breed health, hosting events for the breed, and more. www.amrottclub.org

American Society for the Prevention of Cruelty to Animals: The ASPCA was the first humane organization in North America. Its mission, as stated by Henry Bergh in 1866, is "to provide effective means for the prevention of cruelty to animals throughout the United States." www.aspca.org

American Veterinary Medical Association: This nonprofit association represents more than 80,000 veterinarians and is the accrediting body for American veterinary schools. www.avma.org

ASPCA Animal Poison Control Center: This resource, which is associated with the ASPCA, offers an informative website with lists of pet toxins and FAQs, as well as a hotline for animal poison-related emergencies that is available 24 hours a day, every day, at 888-426-4435. A consultation fee may be charged. www.aspca.org/apcc

Association of American Feed Control Officials: The AAFCO develops and implements uniform and equitable laws, regulations, standards, and enforcement policies for the manufacture, distribution and sale of animal feeds, resulting in safe and useful feeds. www.aafco.org

Association of Pet Dog Trainers: This international organization for professional dog trainers fosters continuing education among its members. www.apdt.com

Canadian Kennel Club: Our northern neighbor's oldest kennel club is similar to the AKC in the States. www.ckc.ca

Canine Freestyle Federation: The CFF's volunteers are devoted to promoting the sport of dancing with dogs and holding demonstrations and competitions under its auspices. www.canine-freestyle.org

Canine Performance Events: An organization that fosters fun and competition through agility trials. www.k9cpe.com

Delta Society: This nonprofit trains and tests therapy-dog teams and aids in the implementation of animal-assisted therapy programs. www.deltasociety.org

Dog Scouts of America: Take your dog to camp. www.dogscouts.com

Fédération Cynologique Internationale: This international canine organization includes eighty-four member countries and partners that all issue their own pedigrees and train their own judges. www.fci.be

Love on a Leash: Share your dog's love with others. www.loveonaleash.org

National Association of Professional Pet Sitters: When you will be away for a while, hire someone to watch and entertain your dog. www.petsitters.org

North American Dog Agility Council: NADAC was founded in 1993 and holds competitive agility events through its sanctioned clubs. www.nadac.com

North American Flyball Association: NAFA was established in 1984 and is recognized as the world's governing body for the sport of flyball. www.flyball.org

Pet Care Services Association: A nonprofit trade association that includes nearly 3,000 American and international pet-care businesses. www.petcareservices.org

Pet Sitters International: This group's mission is to educate professional pet sitters and promote, support, and recognize excellence in pet sitting and to provide reliable pet sitters. www.petsit.com

Rottweiler Rescue: The American Rottweiler Club hosts this site that provides information on Rottweiler rescues and dogs in need throughout the United States and Canada. www.rottnet.net

NOTABLE & QUOTABLE

The tagline for the AKC Canine Good Citizen Program is "Responsible Owners, Well-Mannered Dogs." While every dog needs training and a responsible owner, this is critical for Rottweilers because the breed is often the target of breed-specific legislation. Earning the CGC certification with your Rottweiler teaches your dog good manners and helps him earn a good reputation.

— Mary R. Burch, PhD., director of the AKC Canine Good Citizen Program

When you board your dog, bring enough of his food for his entire stay. Include detailed instructions on how much to feed him, or you can put each of his meals in individual packages. By keeping him on the same diet and feeding schedule, there's less chance of intestinal upset. Pack along his favorite blanket and a few toys to ease the transition.

Skyhoundz: This organization hosts the largest international competitive series of disc-dog events, sells disc-dog gear, and offers disc-dog training information. www.skyhoundz.com

Therapy Dogs International: This volunteer organization tests and certifies dog-and-owner therapy teams. www.tdi-dog.org

United Kennel Club: Established in 1898, this international purebred registry emphasizes performance events and education. www.ukcdogs.com

United States Dog Agility Association: This international organization founded in 1986 introduced the sport of agility to America; its Grand Prix tournament is one of the most prestigious competitions in the sport. www.usdaa.com

World Canine Freestyle Organization: This nonprofit promotes canine freestyle around the world for competition and entertainment. www.worldcaninefreestyle.org

WHILE YOU'RE AWAY

As much as you'd like to bring your Rottweiler along on the family vacation, sometimes that's not possible, and you'll need to arrange for his care while you're gone. If you're thinking about boarding your dog at a kennel, ask your veterinarian or dog-owning friends for recommendations to reputable facilities.

Call prospective kennels to ask questions about prices and services offered before making a reservation for your dog. Ask if the dogs have individual indoor-outdoor runs or stay in a cage-free environment. Depending on your dog's comfort level around a group of new dogs, you may have a preference for a certain type of boarding.

When you find a boarding kennel that meets your needs, schedule an appointment to tour the facilities. Ask to see where the dogs are kept, and take note of the overall cleanliness and upkeep. Make sure that there are no offensive odors and that there is adequate ventilation, heating, and air conditioning. The outdoor runs should have fresh water available and be securely enclosed and covered to protect your Rottweiler from the elements.

Meet some of the employees and ask about their qualifications and their experience with Rottweilers. Observe how much time and attention staff members devote to the dogs' care. Inquire if someone remains at the facility after hours, if there's an evacuation plan in case of an emergency, and if there's a veterinarian on call.

Find out the kennel's policy on required vaccinations, as these protect dogs from contagious illnesses. Kennels require dogs to be current on all core vaccines, as well as rabies, parainfluenza, and kennel cough.

Another option is to hire a pet sitter or dog walker to care for your Rottie in your absence. Some Rottweilers, particularly older ones, feel more comfortable staying in their own homes with pet sitters than going to boarding facilities. The pet sitter will give your Rottie supervision and attention while maintaining his regular diet, exercise, and

grooming routines. You won't have to rely on friends or family for help, and you'll have a secure feeling that your dog is well cared for by a professional.

When looking for a responsible pet sitter, interview candidates carefully. Ask about their experience with large-breed dogs and check their references. Find out what services they offer. Will they come by several times a day for walks, exercise, potty breaks, feeding, and companionship? Will they stay overnight at your home with your dog? Will they provide house-sitting services, too, such as watering plants and bringing in the mail? Do they work with others who can care for

your dog if they're unable to? Do they know canine first aid, and what would they do if a medical emergency arises?

Once you've narrowed down your choices, arrange to meet potential candidates before you make a final decision. Observe your Rottweiler's rapport with the sitters and how they respond to your dog.

When you choose a pet sitter, you'll need to provide them with complete instructions. Write down what the sitter needs to know about your dog's personality, daily routine, meals, and any medical conditions. Be sure to leave contact information for your regular vet and the nearest after-hours emergency clinic. To locate a reputable pet sitter, contact the National Association of Professional Pet Sitters (www.petsitters.org). This non-profit organization certifies dedicated professionals who are experienced in canine behavior, nutrition, health, and safety.

PUPPY KINDERGARTEN

Enrolling your Rottweiler in puppy kindergarten classes provides excellent early socialization in a structured setting for puppies between three and six months of age. These help prepare him for later learning by introducing him to other dogs and people.

These classes are usually offered weekly, so it's important to take your puppy to other places in your community the rest of the week to help your dog become accustomed to other sights and sounds. Schedule some time before or after your workday to walk your dog around outdoor malls, garden centers, home renovation stores, the carwash, or any place that accepts dogs.

For really active Rottweiler puppies that may get into mischief when left alone, consider doggie day care. These facilities offer training, playtime, or grooming services. Interview these facilities as carefully as you would a boarding kennel or in-home pet sitter. As expensive as doggy day care may be, it's often less than the cost of replacing your furniture or possessions if your dog destroys them due to boredom.

TAGS, CHIPS, AND GPS

Your Rottweiler should always wear a proper-fitting collar with an ID tag that includes your name and phone number. As a backup measure if the collar or tag ever falls off, a microchip permanently identifies your dog.

A microchip is a small electronic chip enclosed in a glass cylinder that is about the size of a grain of rice. The veterinarian injects the microchip under the dog's skin at the top of the dog's shoulder blades. It is no more painful than a typical injection. The chip contains an identification number that is registered to you; many veterinarians, animal shelters, and police departments are equipped with hand-held scanners that can read microchips.

To do its job, the chip must be registered with a national database. It's important to keep your information current so that your dog can be reunited with you if he ever becomes lost.

New GPS-enabled dog tracking systems enable owners to track and precisely locate their lost or stolen dogs. A small, lightweight, water-resistant locator attaches to the dog's collar within a secure pouch. Using a cell phone or computer, owners can track their dogs. This is not a foolproof way to keep track of your dog, as the batteries must be frequently recharged, the range may be limited, and collars can be

NOTABLE & QUOTABLE

Between 6 and 8 million pets enter animal shelters in the United States each year. This includes many lost family pets. To make it easy for pet owners to play an active role in helping lost pets get home quickly, they can now check their phones or iPods. There's a free iPhone/iPod app called PetRescuers by HomeAgain.

—Gary MacPhee, Director and General Manager, HomeAgain

removed. This high-tech device is simply one more way to identify your Rottweiler.

ROTTIE ROAD TRIP

Rottweilers are great traveling companions. They never ask, "Are we there yet?" They don't get mad if you miss an exit or get lost. Plus, they're always up for some fun.

Take your Rottie on frequent short car rides before planning a big trip so he can become accustomed to the motion. The safest way for your Rottie to travel is in his crate or buckled into a doggy safety harness. Do not let him ride loose in the car, as he will have no protection and can become seriously injured if you're ever in an accident.

Plan ahead for your dog's comfort by packing a bag that contains enough dog food, plus a little extra, for your trip. You may not be able to purchase your regular brand once you're on the road. Bring his leash, a food and water dish, a few favorite toys, dog shampoo, a brush, and some treats. If he requires medication, make sure that you have enough for the trip's duration; bring a copy of the prescription if you'll need to refill it. A copy of your dog's vaccination and other medical records comes in handy if your dog needs emergency veterinary treatment. Make sure that your dog's ID tag and microchip are up-to-date with the correct information.

Don't forget plastic bags for cleaning up after your dog and a roll of paper towels in case of any accidents or motion sickness in the car. It's also a good idea to carry bottled water or a large water container from home. Water systems contain different chemicals, so bringing along the water that he's used to will help prevent gastrointestinal upset.

Schedule plenty of rest stops along the way so that your Rottie can stretch his legs and have potty breaks. Never leave your dog alone in a locked car. The temperature inside a car rises quickly, and your Rottweiler can succumb to heatstroke in a matter of minutes.

INDEX

ROTTWEILER, a Smart Owner's Guide®
part of the Kennel Club Books® Interactive Series®

LIBRARY OF CONGRESS CATALOGING-IN-PUBLICATION DATA

Gewirtz, Elaine Waldorf.
Rottweiler / by Elaine Waldorf Gewirtz
     p. cm. -- (Smart owner's guide)
ISBN 978-1-59378-781-3
1. Rottweiler dog.
SF429.R7G49 2012
636.73--dc23

                              2011031139

JOIN **Club Rottie™** TODAY!